BUILDING A BUZZ

BUILDING A BUZZ

Libraries & Word-of-Mouth Marketing

PEGGY BARBER AND LINDA WALLACE

AMERICAN LIBRARY ASSOCIATION
CHICAGO 2010

Prior to launching Library Communication Strategies, a consulting firm for libraries, in 2000, **Peggy Barber** was associate executive director for communication for the American Library Association (ALA), where she established the ALA Public Information Office, Public Programs Office, and the ALA Graphics program, including the widely known celebrity READ poster series. She is coauthor with Linda D. Crowe of *Getting Your Grant: A How-to-Do-It Manual for Librarians* (Neal-Schuman, 1993). Barber received the Lippincott Award in 1999 and was honored as Alumni of the Year in 2001 by the Rutgers University School of Library and Information Science. **Linda Wallace** is cofounder and partner of Library Communication Strategies. She was formerly director of the ALA Public Information Office, where she developed and implemented creative strategies for National Library Week, Library Card Sign-Up Month, Teen Read Week, and many other public awareness campaigns. Wallace is the author of *Libraries, Mission, and Marketing: Writing Mission Statements That Work* (American Library Association, 2004). She has written and edited many other ALA publications, including the Campaign for America's Libraries @ your library toolkits for public, school, and academic libraries. Wallace received two Addys and two John Cotton Dana special awards for her work as community relations coordinator for the Mideastern Michigan Library Cooperative and was named Librarian of the Year by the Flint Area Library Association.

While extensive effort has gone into ensuring the reliability of information appearing in this book, the publisher makes no warranty, express or implied, on the accuracy or reliability of the information, and does not assume and hereby disclaims any liability to any person for any loss or damage caused by errors or omissions in this publication.

The paper used in this publication meets the minimum requirements of American National Standard for Information Sciences—Permanence of Paper for Printed Library Materials, ANSI Z39.48-1992. ∞

Library of Congress Cataloging-in-Publication Data
Barber, Peggy.
    Building a buzz : libraries and word-of-mouth marketing / Peggy Barber and Linda Wallace.
        p. cm.
    Includes bibliographical references and index.
    ISBN 978-0-8389-1011-5 (alk. paper)
    1. Libraries—Marketing. 2. Libraries—Public relations. 3. Libraries—United States—Marketing—Case studies. I. Wallace, Linda K. II. Title.
Z716.3.B37 2010
021.7—dc22

                                                                          2009025146

ISBN-13: 978-0-8389-1011-5

Printed in the United States of America
PODv1

Contents

Preface

Word-of-mouth marketing (WOMM) makes sense for libraries for many reasons. You'll find out why in this book. You'll also find powerful tools and techniques to help get people talking about your library and some great examples of how WOMM can work for all types of libraries.

Following many years of adventures in library promotion at the American Library Association, we "graduated" in 2000 and soon after launched a consulting practice, Library Communication Strategies. Our mission: to support libraries of all types with creative, practical, and effective communication strategies.

We'd been buzzing about buzz for some time when two regional library systems in Illinois, the DuPage Library System (DLS) and the North Suburban Library System (NSLS), applied for and received a Library Services and Technology Act (LSTA) grant to provide training, planning support, and information resources on word-of-mouth marketing. Thirty-five libraries participated, including twenty-nine public, three academic, two school, and one special. We were hired to lead the training sessions and provide counsel on project development. It was a learning experience for all of us, and we wrote this book in the hope that you, too, will benefit.

Our thanks to all the libraries that participated in the Buzz Grant marketing project and most especially to Sharon Ball, Judy Hoffman, Mary Witt (NSLS), Renee Anderson, and Denise Zielinski (DLS), the masterminds behind this project.

We know you're busy, so we've tried to be brief. As Judy beautifully summarized—

One 2007 LSTA Grant +

Two Illinois Library Systems +

Two Library Marketing Gurus +

Thirty-five Pioneering Libraries =

One Big BUZZ of a Practical, Powerful BOOK.

We hope you'll agree, and we look forward to hearing your questions, successes, and challenges. E-mail us at librarycomm@librarycomm.com.

Happy buzzing!

Acknowledgments

A special thanks to all who shared their insights and experiences for this book, especially our contributors:

Renee Anderson, Marketing Specialist, DuPage Library System, Geneva, Illinois

Joyce Fedeczko, Information Services Director, BP Information Services, Naperville, Illinois

Judy Hoffman, Marketing/Communications Specialist, North Suburban Library System, Wheeling, Illinois

Juli Janovicz, Head of Adult Services, Winnetka-Northfield (Illinois) Public Library District

Rosemary Kauth, Circulation and Technical Services Coordinator, Zion-Benton Public Library, Zion, Illinois

Beth Keller, Marketing Specialist, Highland Park (Illinois) Public Library

Jeanné Lohfink, District Librarian, Beach Park School District, Lake County, Illinois

Erin Maassen, Public Relations Manager, Cook Memorial Public Library District, Libertyville, Illinois

Jane Malik, Assistant Professor, Library Services, Oakton Community College and College of Lake County, Des Plaines, Illinois

Nancy Maloney, Electronic Resources Librarian, BP Information Services, Naperville, Illinois

Kathryn I. Martens, Library Director, Crystal Lake (Illinois) Public Library

Ann McDonald, Marketing Associate, Glen Ellyn (Illinois) Public Library

Carolynn Muci, Marketing/Public Relations Director, Mount Prospect (Illinois) Public Library

Dwayne Nelson, Youth Services and Reference Librarian, Town and Country Public Library, Elburn, Illinois

Debbie Potocek, Technical Services Associate, Zion-Benton Public Library, Zion, Illinois

Sally Schuster, Public Relations Coordinator, Addison (Illinois) Public Library

Elizabeth Stearns, Assistant Director, Community Services, Waukegan (Illinois) Public Library

Uri Toch, Librarian, Reference and Instruction, Oakton Community College and College of Lake County, Des Plaines, Illinois

Susan Westgate, Assistant Director, Bartlett (Illinois) Public Library

Sandy Whitmer, Library Director, Warrenville (Illinois) Public Library

Judy Wright, Head of Circulation, Winnetka-Northfield (Illinois) Public Library District

Denise Zielinski, Director of Informational Services, DuPage Library System, Geneva, Illinois

CHAPTER 1

Word of Mouth versus Word-of-Mouth Marketing

Notice. The title of this book is *Building a Buzz: Libraries and Word-of-Mouth Marketing*—not just word of mouth. That's because we're talking about more than talking. Before we focus on building a buzz, we must put it in the larger context of marketing.

WHAT IS MARKETING?

For a very long time, many of our colleagues resisted business-world strategies like advertising and marketing. They believed that "If we build it, they will come" and thought commercial tools were beneath their dignity. Wow . . . How times have changed. Libraries today face huge competition both for users and support. And there is growing interest in marketing and communication for libraries.

Marketing is all about three things: Getting *organized, focused*, and *consistent* in how we deliver the service and how we communicate. Our favorite definition comes from marketing gurus Philip Kotler and Sidney Levy:

> Marketing is that function of the organization that can keep in constant touch with the organization's consumers, read their needs, develop products that meet these needs, and build a program of communications to express the organization's purposes.[1]

This definition makes it clear that marketing is . . .

- *about listening*—not just telling or selling. It is two-way communication.
- *about them*—not us. We build our collections and services based on what our community/school/university/business wants and needs.
- *about people*—not stuff. We can't just reel off a list of our impressive inventory and expect anyone to care.

WHY YOU NEED A PLAN

If we're going to get organized, stay focused, and be consistent, we need a plan—one that everyone can see and understand. The marketing plan is an essential tool that will help you make the most productive use of your time, energy, and dollars. Marketing is a mind-set as much as an activity. The library director and

> *The most successful part of our project is the marketing plan itself. The fact that we sat down and finally drafted a plan has been a huge boon for us. It has helped us identify what we are doing well as well as what we could be doing better.*
>
> —Kelly Watson, director, Bensenville (Illinois) Community Public Library

board must make marketing a priority at the highest level, realizing that we are free to pick and choose the commercial techniques that work for us. We're in charge. We can make it happen. As nonprofit organizations, libraries are mission driven, market dependent.

Marketing is a team sport. To get started, we suggest the director appoint a core marketing team—not more than six or eight people—to develop a marketing plan. The director must be involved, but there should also be interested staff from all levels. You may also want to include representatives of your board or Friends. When your team members contribute their experience and wisdom to the plan, they will own it and become its vital spokespeople.

There are many fat texts that define and discuss how to develop a marketing plan. The following outline identifies four key elements—research, plan, communicate, and evaluate—and suggested steps in developing a marketing plan, a good agenda for your marketing team.

Marketing Plan Key Elements

1. Research: Analyze the situation and get the facts (primary and secondary research). Listen.

    A. Describe the community, including demographic characteristics and trends.
    B. Describe the library, including staff, support, governance, circulation trends, and so forth.
    C. Define your audience (market segments) and their needs. Gather information on their wants and needs. Research may include many strategies—from conducting surveys and focus groups to taking people to lunch and listening.

2. Plan: Set strategic goals, determine measurable objectives, and develop service strategies.

    A. Start with the library's mission.
    B. Develop services and delivery methods to meet identified needs and wants—also desires.
    C. Develop a positioning strategy. What do you offer that the competition doesn't?

3. Communicate: Identify strategies for two-way communication.

    A. Develop a communication plan with action steps and a timetable. Establish a budget and assign tasks.
    B. Focus on listening to key markets and audiences.
    C. Develop tools such as a basic fact sheet for the library, campaign press kit, talking points, and so forth.
    D. Build a press/contact list of media and opinion leaders and use it.
    E. Develop a media plan with a time line for sending releases and placing stories and public service messages.

4. Evaluate: How are we doing? Are objectives being met?

    A. Set up evaluation procedures.
    B. Measure performance versus plan and adjust accordingly.

COMMUNICATION CHECKLIST

Ideally, your planning activity should start with a communication audit, an objective analysis by an outside observer, of all the ways the library is communicating—everything from the annual report to how the telephone is answered. Internal communication should be included. It isn't easy to self-evaluate, but the following checklist will help. Use it to help answer these questions:

- *Is this library welcoming?*
- *What is our message?*
- *What is our style?*
- *How do we listen?*

1. **Accessibility**—Can people with disabilities or baby carriages easily navigate the library building and website?

2. **Brand/identity**—Does the library have a clear and consistent image—in print, in person, online? This includes consistent use of logo and full location info (including URL).

3. **Customer service**—Is the library's commitment to excellent customer service reflected in the courtesy and helpfulness shown to customers? Are there clearly defined policies and guidelines? Are there ID tags for staff? Do staff members receive timely information and training?

4. **Listening**—Do frontline staff provide feedback on customer wants, complaints, compliments? Are all staff members encouraged to listen and provide feedback on what they hear? Are there opportunities for customers to give input in the library and online?

5. **Decor, decoration**—Is the library too light or too dim? Is the library clean and clutter free? Is there effective use of posters, banners, art, and other promotional opportunities such as screen savers?

6. **Display**—Are books and other materials displayed face out? Are there "shelf talkers"?

7. **Local ownership**—How well does the library reflect the community, including its diversity? Is there a bulletin board? Displays of local art? Are there opportunities for the users to give feedback on library service, interact with other users, share their comments on books?

8. **Message**—Does your library have a key message? Do staff members know and communicate the message? How else is it communicated? Bookmarks and fliers? Letterhead and business cards? Newsletters?

9. **Media**—Does your library have a presence in relevant media? Is someone assigned to work with the press? Does your library initiate stories, interviews, and placements of public service announcements and advertising? Is there a media plan?

10. **Outreach**—Does the library have a life outside the building? Does it have a presence in the life of the community?

11. **Programming**—Does the library actively offer and promote programs and training sessions? How are programs promoted?

12. **Print materials**—Are there too many? Too few? Are they attractive? Is there a clear message?

13. **Signage: internal and external**—Is the library easy to find? Is it easy to find what you're looking for? Is the library mission visible? Does signage reflect awareness of diversity?

14. **Telephone**—Does a person or a machine answer the phone? If it's a machine, does your telephone greeting help or harm your image? Is it clear? Easy to follow?

15. **Website**—Is the image/message consistent with other library communications? Does it take advantage of the unique qualities of the Web? Is the website treated as a branch library?

16. **Body language**—What is the unspoken message being delivered by staff?

What other ways is your library communicating? We invite you to add to this list.

THE MARKETING COMMUNICATION PLAN

Most libraries have strategic service plans, but few have communication plans. A true marketing plan includes a communication plan—one that supports the library's overall service goals and objectives. You also can and should have marketing communication plans that focus on specific audiences, services, or programs. The next tool we're giving you is an eight-step outline for your marketing communication plan. It's simple, logical (each step builds on the other), and it works. A sample plan is included in the "Power Pack," chapter 6.

Eight Steps to Success

Use this outline as a map for developing your plan.

1. **Introduction** (Briefly explain why you are proposing this plan. Identify strengths, weaknesses, opportunities, and threats [SWOT]. Include relevant research and observations.)

2. **Communication goals** (The dream. Big picture. No more than three goals.)

3. **Objectives** (Three to five doable, measurable outcomes.)

4. **Positioning statement** (What is your unique selling proposition? What do you want people to think and feel about the library? Example: "The library is the best first stop for expert help in connecting children and youth to learning and discovery." —State Library of North Carolina)

5. **Key message** (What is the most important thing you want people to know/do? In ten words or less plus three talking points that support it.)

THE BUZZ ABOUT BUZZ

Interview with Judy Hoffman

Judy Hoffman, marketing communications specialist for the North Suburban Library System, managed the buzz project for that system.

What do you think was the best thing that came out of the project?

Libraries learned the power of an informed and engaged staff. Libraries also came to recognize that marketing is everyone's job. They experienced that marketing can be as easy as a smile and a conversation—be it at the circulation desk or the checkout line at the grocery store.

Have you observed any changes in how the participating libraries do things?

I hear much less moaning that a library can't do marketing because of lack of funding. Also, these libraries seem much less hesitant to try something new. Of great importance, they truly understand the need to start their promotions with a plan and to have measurable goals and objectives.

How would you describe the response to the Buzz Grant project?

Libraries were hungry for marketing help. While there might have been some skepticism, that didn't dampen their curiosity. The introductory buzz marketing program, which was open to all libraries as part of the grant, drew a huge crowd. By the end of that one session, the libraries were clamoring to come on board. Peggy Barber and Linda Wallace presented the basics in such a way that it *just made sense.*

Libraries were excited to build on their grant projects or apply the techniques to a new effort. People seemed to enjoy the challenge and often commented that they found it fun. A number of libraries that had not participated in the grant asked for more opportunities for training and advice on how to launch their own projects. The buzz marketing website, with all thirty-two project reports and other resources, is often referred to as a valuable resource.[2]

Anything you would do differently in terms of the grant process?

While the time frame (eight months) seemed short, it worked to the advantage of the project. The small window forced a more focused approach than many libraries might have had with a longer time frame.

Any other wisdom about word-of-mouth marketing to share?

I have the honor of serving as a judge for the American Library Association John Cotton Dana Public Relations Awards. Reading the many wonderful award submissions, I was pleased to see that in 2008, many libraries throughout North America are including word-of-mouth marketing as an integral component of their marketing plans. The realization has spread that this is a technique that has always been a key to success for marketing in both the commercial and nonprofit world. This "under-the-radar" tactic is now a studied powerhouse that is being used more creatively and effectively than ever.

6. **Key audiences** (External and internal. Be specific.)

7. **Strategies/tactics/tools** (How will you deliver the message? Core strategies include partnerships, media publicity, displays, programming, special events, website/e-mail, direct mail, and outreach, for example, parades and presentations, word of mouth, etc. Develop an action plan and budget.)

8. **Evaluation measures** (How will you know what worked and what didn't? Refer back to your objectives.)

Notes

1. Philip Kotler and Sidney Levy, "Broadening the Concept of Marketing," *Journal of Marketing* 33 (January 1969): 15.

2. "What's the Buzz? Word of Mouth Marketing and Libraries," North Suburban Library System, www.nsls.info/resources/marketing/buzzmarketing/default.aspx.

CHAPTER 2

The Power of Word-of-Mouth Marketing

Getting people to talk often, favorably, to the right people in the right way about your product is far and away the most important thing that you can do as a marketer.

—George Silverman,
The Secrets of Word-of-Mouth Marketing

WHY IT WORKS

Think about it. What makes you decide to try a new restaurant, see a particular movie, or read a novel? Is it because you saw an ad, or because a friend—someone you trust—recommended it?

There is no more powerful communication technique than the simple act of one person talking to another. In this section we'll talk about why.

With all the newfangled technology out there, the commercial world is turning to word-of-mouth marketing (WOMM) as the most powerful form of advertising. This is great news for libraries because WOMM *is* truly powerful and because *we can afford it.* For the first time, the playing field is level. We can compete. We can win public awareness and support.

For a general introduction, we recommend George Silverman's *The Secrets of Word-of-Mouth Marketing.*[1] Silverman's book is a good and inspirational read (yes . . . we're doing WOMM here). The quote in the epigraph (at left) is one of our favorites.

Today, the whole advertising arena has totally changed. Today there are so many more choices and so much clutter. We're no longer all watching the same TV shows. One study says the average person is exposed to 3,000 advertising messages in a day.[2] It sounds like a lot until you think about all the ads you see and hear in newspapers and magazines, in the mail, and on TV and radio, billboards, and your computer screen. American companies spend more on advertising than Mexico's entire gross domestic product—more than $230 billion each year.[3]

During an average evening of TV, you'll see about 128 ads.[4] Do you remember when one of the benefits of cable television was the absence of advertising? Do you remember when a commercial break on a television show was two thirty-second advertisements? We invite you to count them now. You may see six or more, not including the announcements of upcoming programs. Do the ads get your attention? Do you remember them? Do you run out and buy the products? Or start worrying about all the scary side effects of those prescription drugs? You probably zone out on the ad marathons, TiVo past them, or head for the kitchen. But chances are you'll remember—and believe—what your friends tell you.

A few years ago, Linda was driving down a busy Chicago street behind a van that said, "When Your Plumbing's Dead, Call Ed." That poetic message got her attention. She still remembers it to this day. But who did she call when her plumbing did die? It wasn't Ed. Instead, she asked a friend to recommend a good plumber. *That* is the power of word-of-mouth marketing.

Starbucks. The Body Shop. And eBay. These are all companies that built their reputations on the strength of their product and strategic use of word of mouth. Satisfied customers became their sales force. Positive word of mouth is so simple, basic, and powerful that it's hard to imagine any company prospering without it. And you can probably think of more than a few ventures (we won't name them) that have suffered from negative word of mouth. You also may have heard that some companies are paying people to do word of mouth for them. This is *not* the kind of word of mouth we are talking about, and it is considered unethical in the advertising profession.

Word-of-mouth marketing works best when it is genuine and reflects true passion. One of our favorite bits of wisdom about WOMM comes from Guy Kawasaki, who had the title of chief evangelist for Apple Computer. Guy says:

> Any car manufacturer should go to the Harley Davidson biker rally. They would learn a lot. It's almost too obvious. I'd like to know: How many car manufacturers have sent their marketing staff to a HOG (Harley Owners' Group) rally? They would learn a shitload of stuff. Pardon my French.[5]

Why is this quote important? Because it prompts a big question. Could the people who use your library become a passionate community of champions? Even if they don't wear leather? Could library users get as wound up and committed as Harley riders? Could they have as much fun? We think it's not only possible but essential. Word-of-mouth marketing can make it happen.

So why is WOMM so powerful? It comes down to five things.

1. It's real and immediate—real, live people telling other people in real time.

2. It's personal—not a pitch. The person knows you and is trying to be helpful.

3. It's honest. There's no commission, no connection. You're more likely to believe.

4. It's catching. People love to share a good idea or experience, and other people love to listen. In fact, there's only one thing people like to share more than a good experience—a bad experience.

5. It's customer-driven. The customer determines when she/he will talk/listen. It is not imposed.

TURNING CUSTOMERS INTO CHAMPIONS

The commercial world is buzzing about the power of word-of-mouth marketing, and there are some special reasons why library land should be even more enthused. We think the pyramid in figure 2.1, from *Word-of-Mouth Marketing*, by Jerry R. Wilson, is an excellent model for thinking about the people we serve or wish to serve.[7]

Who are these people and why should we care? We believe the answers, adapted for libraries, can help us communicate smarter and get better results.

Suspects: individuals who don't think about the library; the library is not part of their lives

Prospects: individuals who might become library users if someone encourages them to

Customers: individuals who use the library, if only occasionally

Clients: individuals who use the library on a regular basis and often have a relationship with library staff

Champions: individuals who use the library, have a relationship with library staff, advocate for the library (without being asked!), and maybe give money

Clearly, the champions are the influential big hitters who can help make the library part of mainstream conversation throughout the community. This concept is especially potent for libraries because of our huge number of customers. Rather than investing all our energy into reaching every last suspect and prospect, it makes sense to focus on moving our customers up the pyramid to become clients and champions. We've used this pyramid in workshops for librarians and have seen it start the wheels turning. We'd like you to start thinking about it, too. *How can we turn our customers into champions?*

More things to consider:

Libraries have huge numbers of customers. A recent Harris poll found about two-thirds (68 percent) of Americans own a library card and that three-quarters (76 percent) of them visited their libraries last year. Almost all Americans (92 percent) say they view their local library as an important education resource.[8] Impressive numbers? Absolutely! Nearly every day there are stories in the media about how libraries are busier than ever. What is your library's daily door count? We ask this question and are continually amazed by what we hear. Whether it's a public, school, or academic library, the numbers of daily visitors would make most any retailer jealous.

What's the difference between a customer and a client? The answer is simple. Clients have a relationship. Many librar-

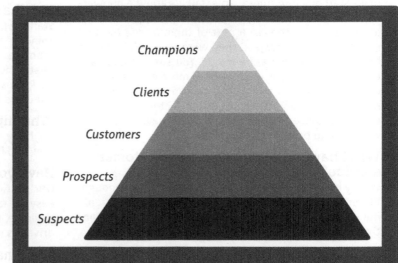

FIGURE 2.1 WOMM can help us move people from the bottom to the top of this pyramid.

Reproduced with permission of John Wiley and Sons.

ians used to believe that acquiring and organizing information and opening the doors were enough. If that's all we do, the encounter between the library and the customer will be totally transactional. They'll find what they want or not. We'll never know. There is still some feeling among our colleagues that it is improper to have a relationship with our customers, that we should not interfere. We also hear that some library staff think getting to know or be known by customers is potentially dangerous. It seems the addition of new technology has changed or is changing this old relationship resistance. Public librarians used to say, "We don't teach." Now staff are helping people learn to use computers, apply for jobs, file for unemployment, and find other vital information using the Internet. Relationships are happening, and with deliberate encouragement, clients can be turned into champions who tell their friends to use and support their library.

Libraries already have champions, but there is huge potential to increase their numbers and encourage activism. We encourage you to take inventory of the library family. For most public libraries this includes staff, board members, Friends, and volunteers—and for some, library foundation board members and staff. When all these folks become active buzzers, the word about library pro-

THE BUZZ ABOUT BUZZ

Interview with Juli Janovicz

Juli Janovicz, head of adult services at the Winnetka-Northfield (Illinois) Public Library District, became a buzz fan after her library's successful venture in promoting online resources. (See "WOMM at Work: Reports from the Front Lines," chapter 5.)

What's so great about WOMM?

People are always looking for the magic pill that will make staff buy into things. This is it! It's about empowerment. We undertake big projects, but library staff don't always feel like they're a part of them or see the end results. With this project, they were part of it from the beginning. And that's the magic. You see the database use increase, but you also see staff morale increase. The excitement builds, and as the patrons come back and report how they've been using the materials at home, the process keeps building and we're having fun. And work should be about having fun.

What have you learned about customer service?

We try not to make people angry, but that's not enough. When people have a bad experience, it travels fast. It's not enough just to be nice. They have to have a substantive good experience beyond being nice.

Why do you think WOMM is important for libraries?

Complacency isn't going to do. Eighty-five percent of our residents are cardholders, but we can't afford to be complacent.

What was the most challenging part?

Making the pieces fit together so that staff could make the leap from customer service to marketing. Marketing is something we do every day. Every time we talk to patrons we are marketing the library. Staff needed to believe that their conversations at the circulation desk were an integral part of boosting the online statistics.

What was most rewarding?

People are coming back and saying thanks for showing them resources they can use.

What did you learn from this project?

Incentives work.

How has staff responded?

Staff are proud of their role, and they are listening more. They see word of mouth working. They see results. We promote our online resources all the time, so our patrons relate their experiences, both positive and negative, back to us. This ongoing channel of communication with our users is invaluable.

What tips would you give to others?

Anybody can do it. It's so easy. It should be a conversation, and it has to be librarywide.

Have you buzzed about anything else?

Our next campaign was about our new website. It was easy to talk about a beautiful website with easy-to-navigate pages and resources. We gave away flash drives as icebreakers and incentives for patrons.

What has been your director's response?

He has been extremely supportive. You need to have top-down support for a campaign that involves the entire staff. If you want frontline staff to market, you need to have buy-in from all levels of management.

What kinds of changes have you made as a result of what you and the staff have learned about WOMM?

We're making a leap from customer service to marketing. This is what we do: we engage people in conversation. I recently held refresher buzz workshops about new databases for all staff members. A laptop has become a permanent fixture at the circulation desk so staff can demonstrate twenty-four-hour resources on the website and the online catalog to parents while engaged in conversation. When we placed the laptop on the desk, it was obvious that it was a conversation starter.

grams and services will be all over the community. Just think about the potential networks of family, friends, work colleagues, churches, schools, and community groups. The possibilities are awesome. Many trustees don't see advocacy or marketing as part of their job. This must change. It must also change for staff, and when you read the field reports in chapter 5, you'll see that library staff can welcome and enjoy this role.

It's important to remember that although our most immediate payoff comes by turning library users and clients into champions, it doesn't end there. We will also reach many more suspects and prospects via channels they listen to and trust—their friends, neighbors, a teacher, a coworker, or a community leader.

Here are some tips for turning your customers into champions.

Greet people by name. We call it the *Cheers* factor. Almost everyone likes to go to a place "where everybody knows your name." Although it may be easier to remember names in a small community, even staff at very large and busy libraries can give a warm welcome to their regulars.

Give them over-the-top great service. It often doesn't take much. Sometimes what we think is routine can amaze our customers. Make a point of recommending books or websites they might enjoy. Offer to get a book through interlibrary loan, or show them how to do online reserves. Provide reference by appointment.

Initiate conversations. Ask them if they liked the book or movie. Do they know about an upcoming program? Offer tips for Internet searching.

Listen. Invite their feedback, and promise to get them a response.

Find ways to make them feel special. Invite them to the preview for the Friends' book sale. Work with community theater and other community groups to get free or discounted tickets. Don't just put them on the counter. Offer them first to your best customers.

Invite their participation. Encourage them to join the Friends or an advisory group. Recruit them for the board.

Be flexible. Show them you're on their side. Empower staff to bend the rules if necessary.

Teach them how to fish. Not literally, of course. But people appreciate being taught how to do things on their own (e.g., do online reserves, download audiobooks, etc.). Libraries have changed and continue to change—a lot. Sometimes people are embarrassed to ask for help.

Be respectful. Offer your services and then leave people alone.

Notes

1. George Silverman, *The Secrets of Word-of-Mouth Marketing: How to Trigger Exponential Sales through Runaway Word of Mouth* (New York: AMACOM, 2001), 6.

2. Entrepreneur, "Marketing and Advertising Statistics," www.entrepreneur.com/encyclopedia/businessstatistics/article82004.html.

3. Mark Hughes, *Buzzmarketing: Get People to Talk about Your Stuff* (New York: Penguin, 1995), 121.

4. Ibid., 122.

5. Ben McConnell and Jackie Huba, "The Evangelist's Evangelist," www.creating customerevangelists.com/resources/evangelists/guy_kawasaki.asp.

6. "Study: Word of Mouth Tops in Clout," *Business Post News,* April 10, 2008.

7. Jerry R. Wilson, *Word of Mouth Marketing* (New York: Wiley, 1991).

8. American Library Association, "New national poll shows library card registration at record high," www.ala.org/ala/newspresscenter/news/pressreleases2008/September 2008/ORSharris.cfm.

CHAPTER 3

How to Build a Buzz

*Get someone else to blow
your horn and the sound
will carry twice as far.*

—Will Rogers

Building the buzz is all about being part of the conversation. It's not just talking. It's also listening. There are endless conversations going on out there—in homes, schools, businesses, at the beach, the golf course, employee cafeterias. It's up to us to start the conversation, to give people something to talk about. If we do it right, others will buzz for us. In this section, you'll learn what it takes.

MUST-HAVES

We like to say that buzzing is easy, but it isn't necessarily simple. Effective word-of-mouth marketing (WOMM) must have these five things:

1. A good product and *great* customer service

2. A plan

3. A clear, conscious, consistent message

4. A prepared and committed sales force

5. People willing to testify

Now, let's take them one at a time . . .

1. A Good Product and *Great* Customer Service

We have a good product. The Harris poll quoted in chapter 2 shows that 92 percent of the American public think libraries are a good and important educational resource. But to get people buzzing, feeling ownership and respect, there must be something more—exceptional customer service. People expect good service, and if they don't get it, they'll probably just never come back. Or if the service is really bad, they'll also enjoy telling *many* people about their horrible experience. The figure most commonly used is that one unhappy customer will tell nine others.[1] That was before the Internet. Imagine what it might be now!

Building a culture of exceptional service is essential for effective word-of-mouth marketing. There are many examples of how this is done in the business world. One frequently mentioned is Nordstrom. Their customer service policy is incredibly strong, simple, and effective.

This faith in the employee is such a contrast to businesses that require their clerks to ask, "Did you find what you're looking for today?" or say some other rote phrase to every person at the cash register. Nordstrom hires people for good people skills, not their ability to run a cash register; provides training; and most of all, empowers their employees to make decisions. In describing their keys to success, company officials say, "Working at Nordstrom is not for everybody. Demands and expectations are high. The people who succeed enjoy working in an unrestricted environment."[2]

We urge you to make customer service a priority and to get staff involved in developing a culture of excellence. Many libraries have had great success by focusing on and requiring good service. The Columbus (Ohio) Public Library has a system known as CLASS (Customers Leaving Appreciative, Satisfied, and Sold).

We learned about CLASS after making a casual and anonymous visit to the library and experiencing over-the-top service. The whole atmosphere was so welcoming and exceptional that we were motivated to call and find out how they make it happen. This customer service training was developed by a team of staff from all levels. Every job in the library has a competency model, and everyone on the staff has an individual development plan. The annual assessment process aligns with their strategic plan, and pay is tied to performance. The whole system has worked so well that they now share it with other libraries. See "Really Good Resources," in chapter 6.

The Baltimore County (Maryland) Public Library (BCPL) calls its customer service philosophy "YES," which stands for

Y—You are BCPL.

E—Every encounter is an opportunity.

S—Service is a partnership.

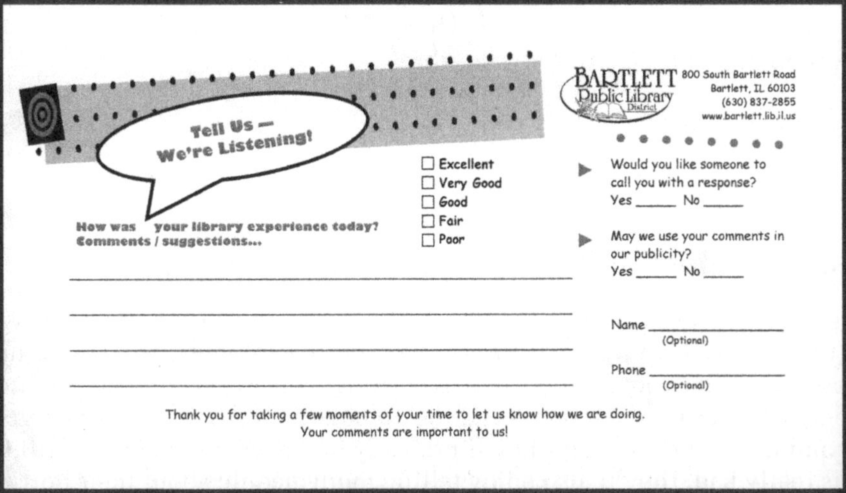

FIGURE 3.1 Customer feedback jumped when the Bartlett (Illinois) Public Library began using this simple form.

Reproduced with permission of the library.

Staff at the West Palm Beach (Florida) Public Library define their customer service style as "The World's Nicest Library." You can see their wallet-sized customer service policy on their website, at www.wpbpl.com. Click on the pop-up "Mildly Delirious Libraries" to learn how this library transformed not only its customer service but its whole image.

There are many more examples, and many books have been written. The bottom line—a culture of exceptional customer service must be built, nurtured, and maintained, and the whole staff must own and be proud of it.

Having great customer relations means being in constant contact with customers. It's not just about great service. It's about listening—asking them what they think and what they want. This can be done with surveys and focus groups, but there are many other ways that don't cost as much and can help you build the buzz (see figures 3.1 and 3.2). We hope our "How to Listen" list will inspire you to come up with even more ways.

2. A Plan

You can't have conscious communication without a plan. The plan is what helps you get organized, stay focused, and be consistent. It's your map, and it helps everyone in the "family" know where you're going.

We encourage you to use/adapt the marketing communication plan outline in chapter 1. It is a useful tool for a library's overall marketing action, and it also works for special projects. Start with a one-year plan. Make it ambitious but doable. What is your dream for the library? What do you want people to know? Who needs to hear the message? How are you going to deliver it? How will you listen? How will you know if the plan is effective? All of these questions are addressed in the eight-step communication plan.

A couple of reminders:

Be sure to include internal audiences and strategies for addressing them in your plan. An objective might be "Our library staff and trustees will feel more skilled and confident in delivering the library's message." Strategies might address how you will build their confidence, listen, and encourage feedback. As part of the evaluation, you might include a very brief pre- and postcampaign survey like the one in the "Power Pack," chapter 6. Good communication starts at home with our library staffs, trustees, Friends, and volunteers. Without their support, your plan is destined to fail.

Also remember that WOMM shouldn't replace other communication strategies, such as media publicity, paid advertising, partnerships, online communication, and so forth. It is the most powerful strategy, but it isn't the only one. Different audiences will respond differently to different messages and strategies. The more ways you listen and deliver your message, the bigger the buzz. Older people still rely more on print media, while younger audiences are plugged into electronic media. Yet another great thing about WOMM is that it works with all audiences. Everyone loves to talk!

One of the best and most important reasons for having a communication plan is that it will save time and money by helping to focus your resources where they will do the most good. In our work with the North Suburban Library System and DuPage Library System in Illinois we saw how having a plan helped libraries to be more organized, focused, and consistent in how they communicate. We also saw that having a limited time frame (the grant period) was a great way to try out WOMM. The participating library teams had to focus on a specific service or target audience or both, set goals and measurable objectives, select a message, identify strategies—and make it happen. It wasn't all easy or

HOW TO LISTEN

- Do what some CEOs do. Call several customers every week and invite their suggestions. Bet they tell their neighbors!

- Even better, take a customer or two to breakfast or lunch every week. Ask them questions. Ask their advice. Listen. Be sure to have a message for them, and ask them to share it with others.

- Create a customer advisory board or several—for adults, teens, and children. Invite their input—and act on it if possible.

- Ask your friends and neighbors what they think about the library; then, listen and report back.

- Encourage your staff to feed back what they hear in- and outside the library—both the good and bad.

- Keep a "No Register." We've heard that staff at some libraries make a note of every time they have to say no to a customer and why. The list is monitored and reviewed to see how no can be turned to yes.

- Place comment boxes prominently throughout the library. Invite positive comments as well as suggestions, and ask if the person would like a response.

- Host a Question/Comments page on your website and post responses.

- Encourage your library board and Friends to listen. The Mount Prospect (Illinois) Library hosts a monthly "Cookies and More with the Board."

Your experience with our team

1. How has the BP Information Services Staff helped you most recently? Please choose one answer below.

○ Supplied requested book or document
○ Sent you a journal table of contents electronically
○ Answered a technical or business question
○ Provided a technical bulletin or business newsletter (such as BP Today, Chemical Industry Newswatch, Fuels Technology Newsletter, etc.)
○ Connected you to an expert
○ Obtained access for you to online information sources like databases, e-journals or e-books
○ Provided lab notebooks or other proprietary information
○ Supplied a safety video for your presentation
○ Other (please specify)

2. What services have you used at other times? Check all that apply.

☐ Book or document ordering
☐ Journal table of contents service
☐ Technical or business reference question answered
☐ Technical bulletin or business newsletter (such as BP Today, Chemical Industry Newswatch, Fuels Technology Newsletter, etc.)
☐ Expert Services (via Guideline, formerly Teltech)
☐ Access to online information sources like databases, e-journals or e-books
☐ Lab notebooks or other proprietary information
☐ Safety Videos
☐ Other (please specify)

3. How did you learn about BP Information Services?

○ Referred by a colleague
○ Someone forwarded a newsletter or bulletin to me
○ Found on the BP intranet
○ Don't recall
○ Other (please specify)

FIGURE 3.2 Surveys such as this one used by BP Information Services, Naperville, Illinois, are one way to listen to your customers.

Reproduced with permission.

perfect, but there was much success and much learned. Having a communication plan contributed greatly to the success of these projects. You can read their reports in chapter 5, "WOMM at Work: Reports from the Front Lines."

3. A Clear, Conscious, Consistent Message

Heard any good messages lately? All of us are exposed to thousands of messages in the course of our daily lives. But how many do you remember? Why? Are any of them from libraries?

Chances are you'll remember commercial messages first. Slogans like "Just do it." "Diamonds are forever." Or "Got milk?" Almost everyone knows "When it rains, it pours," because Morton Salt has been using it since 1914. Think about the ones you remember and why you remember them. Chances are they're simple, often catchy, and have been around a long time. Advertisers know that people must see or hear a message at least seven times for it to register and up to eleven times before they act.[4] Once they have a message that works, they stick with it. Libraries, on the other hand, are inclined to change their message whenever someone gets tired of it or has a better idea. What we typically see is a mishmash of messages on everything from the website, bookmarks, and annual report to brochures.

Every library should have an overall message that is developed as part of its marketing plan. This message should be easy to say and easy to remember—no more than ten words. What is the most important thing you want people to know about your library? It should be something you and your sales force can comfortably say at the circ desk or across the backyard fence. Some people call this the "elevator pitch." If you have only twenty seconds with someone, what would you tell him or her that would be meaningful and memorable? You may also distill it down to even fewer words to use as a tagline, or branding statement, for your library.

Practice saying your message out loud. Can you can say it comfortably? Test it on other staff and members of the public. Is it clear? Can they remember it? One of the Illinois Buzz Grant project participants, Caryn Scimeca, at the Addison (Illinois) Trails High School, reported that testing paid off for her Learning Media Center. The message that staff had come up with—"The ATLMC: a place to Read, Research, Reflect"—did not test well. It was simplified to "It's easy at the ATLMC!" Some of our other favorite messages from the Buzz Grant project follow:

Get Smart about Homework @ www.warrenville.com—Warrenville (Illinois) Public Library

Ask us about YOUR new library—Addison (Illinois) Public Library

See you at the library!—Town and Country Public Library, Elburn (Illinois)

You Have Questions—We Have Answers. Just Ask Us!—BP Information Services, Naperville (Illinois)

We Make It Happen!—Bartlett (Illinois) Public Library

Remember, word of mouth is not a substitute for other strategies. The very best way to make sure your message is heard is to have one message and use it over and over—in conversation, all print materials, the website, T-shirts, skywriting. All staff, trustees, volunteers, and Friends must be on the same page—literally. We suggest developing a message sheet or sample script that your sales force can use to easily start or drop into a conversation. Questions work well for this, especially if they suggest something new or surprising. "Have you tried our new self-check yet?" In addition to your key message, there should be two or three talking points ("It's easy and fast! Let me show you") and perhaps a couple statistics or examples—the more attention getting the better.

You will also want to develop messages and message sheets for special promotions. If you are introducing a new service or program, it's a good idea to attach a fact sheet, Q&A, or other background materials. We've included a sample message sheet that the Winnetka-Northfield (Illinois) Public Library District used for a campaign to increase the use of online databases. You can see the full report in chapter 5.

Meeting your future needs

Which services you would like to know more about, so you can use them in the future?

4. What services would you like to know more about?

☐ Safety videos
☐ Ordering books & documents
☐ Lab notebooks or other proprietary information
☐ Gaining access to online resources such as databases, e-journals or e-books
☐ Electronic Tables of Contents (Journals)
☐ Receiving answers to technical or business questions
☐ Current Awareness services (such as BP Today, Chemical Industry Newswatch, Fuels Technology Newsletter, etc.)
☐ Subject Expert Services (via Guideline, formerly Teltech)
☐ Other (please specify)

About You

Please provide some background information to help us design our services around your needs.

5. What Segment do you work in?

○ Corporate Functions
○ Exploration & Production
○ Gas, Power & Renewables
○ Refining & Marketing

6. What Business Unit are you in?

7. Where are you located?

○ Africa
○ Asia/Pacific
○ Europe
○ Latin America
○ North America
○ Other Region

8. Please tell us about your experience with BP Information Services. Specific suggestions or testimonials about our products and services are most helpful.

Survey Drawing

The BP Information Services group values your input.
We will acknowledge your participation in this survey by sending a small gift and also enter you in a drawing to win one of four Amazon.com gift certificates.

9. Enter your e-mail address below.

Thank You!

We appreciate your feedback. Thanks again!
The BP Information Services Team: You have Questions -- We Have Answers, Just Ask Us!

FIGURE 3.2 (cont.)

Reproduced with permission.

Another basic power tool for WOMM is the phrase "Please tell your friends." Whether you say this in person, make it a link on website pages, or add it to print materials—use it. One of our favorite stories comes from George Silverman, who wrote about Mo Siegel, the founder of Celestial Seasonings (the herbal tea company). When the company was still young, Mo included a note in each box explaining that the young company didn't have a big advertising budget. He asked that people who enjoyed the tea tell their friends.[5] The rest is history. Now think about how many bookmarks libraries have printed. How many times have we asked people to tell their friends?

Which brings us back to where we started. Repetition does make for learning. Because libraries don't have huge advertising budgets, it is all the more important that our message be *clear, conscious,* and *consistent.*

WINNETKA-NORTHFIELD (ILLINOIS) PUBLIC LIBRARY DISTRICT

Key Message

We're Up When You Are! 24 Hours a Day.
www.winnetkalibrary.org

Talking Points

Our website is an online branch library with a wonderful array of resources . . .

- Encyclopedias,
- Financial tools such as *Morningstar*,
- *Tumblebooks*, a cool online storytime for kids,
- . . . and so much more.

The library pays for premium online subscriptions, so you don't have to.

We give you a world of safe, reliable resources beyond the Internet, and you can use them all in your PJs.

All you need is a library card.

We'll be glad to give you a personal tour of the website and find the best tools for you. Come in or call for an appointment.

Statistics

The library has more than 35 online subscriptions and close to 400 online reference books that you can use from home 24 hours a day.

Stories/Examples

Resident Robert Leonard explained his use of the *Historical New York Times* database while researching and writing an article for *Coin World* magazine. He said, "In five hours, without leaving the house, I wrote it and e-mailed it to the editor. This database has value!"

During the middle of the night our most popular online resources are *Morningstar* and the genealogy subscription site *Heritage Quest*.

DON'T FORGET THE "FAMILY"

We mentioned that you need to address internal audiences in your plan. That includes a message for your sales force, and all the same points apply. Keep it simple and use it consistently in your communications.

A key message might be "You have an important role to play in promoting our library!"

Talking points:

- If people are going to use and support their library, they have to know about it.
- Word-of-mouth marketing is the most powerful way of getting our message out.
- It's easy. It can even be fun. And the price is right!

Call to action: Start buzzing!

WHAT DO YOU SAY?

There is another type of message that comes in very handy. Every time you find yourself at a meeting or party and someone asks, "What do you do?" you have a golden opportunity to deliver a strong, positive message about yourself and the library. You should use your library's message, but it's also important to share your personal enthusiasm for your chosen work. Think about it, and have your answer ready. We heard one librarian say, "I wear a tiara and tell stories . . . I'm a children's librarian." When we asked the "What do you do?" question at a recent WOMM workshop, a couple of giggling gals leaned back seductively. One said, "I'm in adult video." The other said, "I get your circulation going." Then the custodian said, "You drop it. I mop it." Have fun. It's great to surprise and delight people when you bring "library" into the conversation.

4. A Prepared and Committed Sales Force

That would be you! Each of us has hundreds of opportunities—on the job and off, with our family, friends, and neighbors—to deliver the message. If you're what we call a true Library Super Salesperson (LSS), you probably do this already. The challenge is to motivate the whole library family to make WOMM part of their lives.

The clerk at the checkout counter, delivery driver, children's librarian, trustees, and Friends—everyone should know the message and feel comfortable delivering it. Providing tools and training is key. If they're going to be motivated, they need to know why it's important and why their role is important. Sharing the marketing communication plan is one way to help them understand. Having clearly defined customer service philosophy and policies also helps.

If the campaign is focused on a particular service, make sure that everyone on your sales force can talk comfortably about it. We are constantly surprised at how many library staff and board members still don't know what a database is. How can they tell their friends and neighbors how great they are if they've never even seen one?

Although administrators must make marketing a priority, middle managers also play a critical role. Employees turn to their immediate supervisor first when they have questions or need guidance. It's important that managers be prepared to act as role models. That includes understanding why word of mouth is important, delivering a consistent message, listening and responding to their staff's concerns, and feeding back their comments to top management.

Frontline staff, who have direct contact with the public, have the most critical role. Whether full-time, part-time, or volunteer, they are the face and voice of the library. In our experience with WOMM in libraries, we have seen that staff really enjoy being involved, informed, and empowered. They also appreciate simple incentives, such as candy or contests with nice prizes. Giving staff at all levels a voice and role in planning the campaign makes for more and better ideas as well as a sense of ownership. Circulation staff, in particular, are well positioned to play a major role. A few years ago, we heard about an effort at the Naperville (Illinois) Public Library with circ staff promoting the adult summer reading program. Participation increased 121 percent, and Circulation Checkout Supervisor Karen Knight reported, "Nearly everyone who was approached agreed to sign up." For more about engaging circ staff, see the interview with Judy Wright, head of circulation at the Winnetka-Northfield (Illinois) Public Library District, later in this chapter.

Also note that when we say listen, we mean to your staff as well as the public. Asking their opinions and inviting their suggestions are key to getting their buy-in. We've included a sample WOMM survey for staff in the "Power Pack," chapter 6.

THE BUZZ ABOUT BUZZ

Interview with Denise Zielinski

Denise Zielinski, director of informational services for the DuPage Library System (DLS), supervised that system's buzz project.

What do you think was the best thing that came out of the project?
There were two. First was the use of word-of-mouth marketing by everyone, regardless of type of library, area of specialization, or department. It was, and is, a tool that everyone can use. The other was the creativity involved in the development of the ideas and the execution.

Have you observed any changes in how the participating libraries do things?
For the libraries in DLS, they are still using the methodology of word-of-mouth marketing but applying it to their customer service training, database marketing, and general library public relations. This is one of those tools that is applicable for everyone in the library and easy to do!

How would you describe the response to the Buzz Grant project?
I think that the participants were eager for something to help them improve the perception of the library and increase library usage. To find word-of-mouth marketing, be able to use it, and be successful without spending a lot was a great motivator. At the conclusion of the projects, the participants were very excited about word of mouth, and the marketing that was done afterward to share the outcomes was enthusiastically received everywhere we went. There were even some libraries that didn't participate and wished they had afterward.

Anything you would do differently in terms of the grant process?
Nothing that I can think of with regard to the process. Our deadlines were quick, which we thought would be a problem but instead were very motivating and worked to get people taking action sooner.

Any other wisdom about word-of-mouth marketing to share?
Don't contemplate doing it—just do it! It is so easy and cost-effective that the results will amaze you!

Having done many staff day workshops on marketing and word-of-mouth marketing, we have seen that an introduction to the concept of WOMM and its power is a good way to begin. You can use this book to develop training for your library staff. A suggested agenda for staff training is provided in the "Power Pack," chapter 6. The scenarios in chapter 6 demonstrate WOMM in action. They're easy to use and fun. Just recruit some hammy volunteers, hand them the scripts, and let them perform. Even better, ask them to write their own scripts. Whether it's "Guys/Gals in the Locker Room," "Testimonial," "Reluctant Student," or "Welcome Neighbor!" these mini dramas help make WOMM real. And yes, they're a little over the top—both to make a point and provide a laugh. Encourage your staff to have fun with them. You'll be amazed by the dramatic talent and enthusiasm.

INSPIRING AND MOTIVATING EMPLOYEES

If done right, word-of-mouth marketing can be fun and motivating for staff. Listen to their suggestions. Cheer them on. Here are more tips for getting everyone to buzz.

- Develop communication and customer service policies with clearly defined goals and guidelines. Keep them simple!

BUZZ MARKETING Q&A

It's natural for staff to have concerns. Try to anticipate and be prepared to address them. Here are some suggested responses.

Q. What is word-of-mouth marketing?
A. Word-of-mouth marketing is simply talking with a purpose. The goal is to get everyone on staff to spread the word about a particular service, such as our new class on doing a job search online. If we do it right, other people will deliver our message for us because we'll ask them to "please tell your friends." People listen to their friends. That's what makes word-of-mouth marketing so powerful.

Q. Don't we have enough to do already? How can you ask us to do one more thing?
A. We know everyone is busy. We also know that a lot of you already talk about the library when you get a chance. We're just asking you to crank it up a notch and use the message sheet to help people understand and support our library. This is important for both them and us, especially in these economic times.

Q. Why do we need to do word-of-mouth marketing? I already tell people about the library.
A. Word-of-mouth marketing is doing what you do anyway but doing it in a way that has more impact. It's also about getting other people to help deliver the library message by asking them to tell their friends. Our goal is to make libraries part of the conversation in our community.

Q. Everyone loves us already. Why do we need to do this?
A. Just because someone checks out books doesn't mean he or she knows about audiobooks or online-research tools. It's up to us to tell them. We have a responsibility to make sure that people understand what they're getting with their tax dollars. We also need you to listen and feed back what you hear so we can learn from our customers.

Q. Why should I tell someone who doesn't live in our service area?
A. Most libraries offer the same basic services. Educating people about what's available helps build understanding and support for all libraries.

Q. What's the best way to start a conversation?
A. Asking a question is an easy way to engage someone. Looking for clues either visual or verbal can help. For instance, if they have school-age kids, you might ask if they know about the library's online homework center. Or you might ask a computer user if she or he knows about the library's classes on Internet searching.

Q. I'm afraid people will think I'm pushy.
A. Try to remind yourself that you're providing a service by telling people what's available to them. People often are glad to get this information! Of course, you need to be respectful. If someone is obviously in a hurry, that's not a good time to engage him or her.

- Provide ongoing training, tips, and tools. Ask them what would help them.
- Listen—and respond personally—to their questions, concerns, and suggestions.
- Remind them how important they are.
- Communicate on a regular basis using all available channels—the staff bulletin board, intranet, e-mail, fliers, and, of course, WOMM. Staff are no different than anyone else. The more they hear the message, the more likely they are to get it.
- Let your staff see you buzzing.
- Encourage staff to share their WOMM experiences —good and bad—at staff meetings.
- Reward their efforts, even baby steps. Stock up on coffee coupons and give them to staff caught doing the WOMM. Compliments are much appreciated, as are small treats like a candy bar or coupon for a free coffee.
- Make it fun! Have a launch party. Have another party to celebrate your success.

ENGAGING TRUSTEES
- Make WOMM part of their "job description."
- Involve them in developing the library's marketing plan.
- Keep them aware and informed of new and changing library services.
- Educate them about their role in speaking out for the library.
- Make sure they know and understand the library's message(s).
- Ask them to listen and report back what they hear.
- Encourage them to use their contacts to help reach influential community members.

5. People Willing to Testify

Testimonials are powerful! Libraries have many satisfied customers. We need to tap into and share their enthusiasm. (See figure 3.3.) The next time you hear someone say something nice about the library, ask him or her to please put it in writing and give you permission to quote it. Use the quotes you collect on your website and in your newsletter, graphics, brochures, news releases, and talks to community groups. Start a "brag board" where you post compliments from your customers. Sharing positive comments is one of the best ways to get people's attention and deliver a powerful message.

Spontaneous testimonials are great, but asking for them is a key WOMM strategy. The Illinois State University in Normal set up a YouTube station on the main floor of the library during National Library Week where students and faculty could stop and say a few words about why they love the library. "We have received wonderful feedback from students, faculty, and even university administration," said Toni Tucker, assistant to the dean of university libraries. "This was very easy to do and took very little time." You can see the videos on the library's home page, at www.library.ilstu.edu, or on YouTube under "Why I love Milner Library."

Jason Pitts, an employee of the Solon Post Office, uses the Solon Public Library's computers over his lunch hour to work on school assignments.

Library computers put to good use by patrons

By Don Ochs
Solon Library Foundation
Board Member

Jason Pitts cites "relaxing, comfortable, and convenient" as the reasons for his frequent use of the Solon Public Library's computers. Jason is at the keyboard during many noon hours and often after his work hours. For the past four-and-a-half years he has worked at the Solon Post Office as a Retail Sales Associate.

Jason is currently enrolled in night classes at Kirkwood/Mt. Mercy College and will soon receive his B.A. degree in Business and Economics.

Jason uses the library's computers for e-mail and for connecting with his friends, but primarily for necessary academic research for class papers, reports, and presentations. Jason's long-term goals are to be either a Postal Inspector or a Criminal Investigator for the Postal Service.

Jason is not the only adult regularly using the library's computers. In the past year, an increasing number of adults are using the computers. Some of these patrons use the public resource for class work, genealogy, e-mail, security banking issues, job searches, vacation planning, and other purposes. Why? Some of these adults have no computer at home or their printer is not working. All say the library's software is more up-to-date than their own.

Less than a year ago, the library had four computers for public use. Many, many students use these in after-school hours. Last spring, Kris Brown, our Solon Library Director, reported to the Foundation that four more computers were needed, but the budget could not provide for the new equipment.

The Solon Public Library Foundation, funded by donations, bequests, grants, and investment income, voted unanimously to buy and install four new computers. Jason Pitts and an increasing number of adults as well as Solon students are benefiting, in important ways, from the Foundation's support.

Our library welcomes all patrons. If you use the computers we hope you, too, find the experience relaxing, comfortable, and convenient.

FIGURE 3.3 Testimonials like this one in the *Solon* (Iowa) *Economist*, February 25, 2009, are powerful.

Reproduced with permission of the publisher.

In New Jersey, the state library has launched a "Tell Us Your Story" campaign with libraries across the state collecting and sharing stories of how the library has transformed lives.[6] A video titled "We love our NJ libraries" is posted on YouTube. As part of the campaign, the Mount Laurel Library created and displayed poster-sized postcards with the question, "What do you love about your library?" Markers were provided for library visitors to fill in their answers. Joan Serpico, special projects manager, reported, "We got tremendous feedback. Twenty-two giant postcards were filled up over the course of the month by hundreds of customers (kids and adults), and they had a good time doing it." But the quest for testimonials didn't stop there. The library also provided beautiful four-color postcards (1,000 cards for $112, plus shipping) with photos of people enjoying various library activities, a list of key services, and the message "Love your library? Tell a neighbor" (see figure 3.4). The library offered to pay postage and mail the cards. Some twenty-five people took the library up on its offer, and many children wrote comments addressed to the library. Altogether, about 500 disappeared during the first month. Serpico said she feels confident they were put to good use and plans to keep them handy.

FIGURE 3.4 The Mount Laurel (New Jersey) Library used postcards to solicit and share testimonials from their users.

Reproduced with permission of the library.

In a previous life, we worked in communications at the American Library Association (ALA). One of our favorite and most successful National Library Week messages was "Libraries Change Lives." This slogan was used from 1993 to 1996. It was the longest we'd ever used the same message, and in hindsight, it could and should have been longer. As part of the campaign, we encouraged librarians to invite members of the public to share stories about how the library changed their lives. Some librarians said, "Oh, no one will do that!" Their reluctance turned to enthusiasm once those stories started coming in. Many wrote to tell us how great it was for staff and board members to experience the appreciation that people felt for their libraries. We collected the stories at ALA and selected an eloquent eight-year-old, Alexandra Johnson, to meet with President Clinton. The daughter of a military man stationed in Philadelphia, Alexandra wrote:

> The library changed my life when I was four years old. When I was four years old, I did not have any books. The preschool I went to had good books, but I could not take them home. So, Mom told me that I could take books out of the public library and bring them back. She told me that they must not get lost, and when I took out books it helped me with my reading. If I did not have a library, I would not know how to read. Books made me smart.[7]

But that is not the end of the story. Years later, Alexandra's mother wrote to tell us that her daughter was valedictorian of her senior class and had a scholarship to college. Stories are powerful. We still tell that story, and we still get teary.

ALA's READ poster series is another wonderful example of the testimonial power libraries possess. From the first READ poster in 1980, with Mickey Mouse and Pluto reading by the fire, to the READ poster software that librarians use today to honor local celebrities, we have seen that just about everybody likes to be associated with America's libraries. Libraries have incredible cachet and can get the very best. Every ALA READ poster has featured original illustration or photography, and none of the celebrities asked for a dime for their participation. Your library can benefit from ALA's star power, but you also can produce your own posters featuring high-profile community figures—legislators, a popular deejay, a beloved athletic coach—using ALA's READ CD (see "Really Good Resources" in our "Power Pack," chapter 6). But don't just put them on a poster. Ask them to help deliver your message. Many people with a platform are glad to use it for a good cause, especially if you put them on a poster.

Referrals are another form of testimonial. Building relationships with staff at schools, child-care centers, the unemployment office, and other agencies are an excellent way to educate their staffs and encourage them to buzz about the library. You could also approach your local newspaper about doing a library column that would feature a photo of a library user and brief text telling what he or she is reading, a favorite website, and a brief testimonial about the library. It could be the mayor one week and a second-grader the next. The circ staff will have suggestions about who to choose. The newspaper will like it because

THE BUZZ ABOUT BUZZ

Interview with Judy Wright

Judy Wright is head of circulation for the Winnetka-Northfield Public Library District. She and other department heads attended the Buzz Grant project training and enthusiastically took it back to their staff.

What impressed you about this project?

Traditionally, circulation staff isn't involved in marketing. Very few libraries allow their circ staff to interact at that level. We were excited about trying something new.

How did your staff respond?

The staff members were terrific. We were excited to see them excited. Some were a little more aggressive than others, but everyone participated. Some of the people I least expected were really shining by the end. I heard them say things like, "It's easy and fun to talk about things you know about and support."

How did you motivate them?

The incentives helped make it fun, but when we gave them training on the databases, that was when it took off. Our staff felt knowledgeable and empowered once they saw how wonderful some of these databases are and how they could serve our patrons. Because they felt it was such a good product, it was easy for them to promote.

What kind of tools and incentives did you use?

There was a contest to come up with a message ("We're Up When You Are! 24 Hours a Day"). Everyone was encouraged to enter. Everyone received a cheat sheet with our message and talking points. We had a bookmark with a checklist so we could mark the ones we showed patrons. We would ask them, "Do you know we have *Morningstar*?" or "Do you know about the Tumblebooks site?" and demo it to them. We would circle the sites on the bookmark so they would remember once they returned home. Also, everyone who received a demonstration was given a notepad with our message. Having something to give out made it easier for the staff to present their message. The two staff who gave out the most notepads at the main library and our branch received gift cards.

Are you still buzzing?

Yes!! We have installed a laptop computer at the circ desk so we could show people the databases. Staff use it to show how to do online reserves and account records as well as demonstrate databases. People like it. We like it. We're educating people more and more about databases and other services available online. It's become an expectation we have for staff. WOMM is being incorporated as a core competency and part of our staff evaluations.

Why do you think WOMM works?

Hearing about and seeing the databases demonstrated makes a lasting impression—more so than seeing it in a newsletter. I think people respect someone else's opinion. You can also convey some excitement speaking one-on-one that you can't in a printed word.

What was the biggest thing you learned?

We learned that this is one of the most successful ways to market. We've had better results from word of mouth than anything we've done—tangible results. We could see the statistics jumping.

What advice would you give other libraries?

Many studies have found that circulation staff are often the first—and sometimes only—contact that patrons have when visiting the library. We miss a lot of opportunities by not encouraging the circ staff to promote the library. Get your circ staff out there. Get them trained and empowered and let them go. It will surprise you!

photos of local folks help sell newspapers. Readers will enjoy looking to see who's featured this week and what he or she has to say—a fun, quick read. We encourage you to work with your local newspaper staff to come up with a format that works both for you and them.

You can also seek out experts, such as newspaper columnists, professors, and business and government leaders, to get extra-special, high-powered quotes. But remember, all your testimonials don't have to be from celebrities or VIPS. Quotes from parents, businesspeople, seniors, immigrants, kids, and teens can have just as much—if not more—impact. All you have to do is ask! We've included some sample testimonials. Your local ones will be even better. People like libraries, but we must push beyond passive positive regard. Using WOMM, we can convert customers to champions.

SAMPLE TESTIMONIALS

"I used to go to the library all the time when I was kid. As a teenager, I got a book on how to write jokes at the library, and that, in turn, launched my comedy career." —*comedian Drew Carey*

"At the moment that we persuade a child, any child, to cross that threshold, that magic threshold into a library, we change their lives forever, for the better." —*President (then Senator) Barack Obama*

"What can I say? Librarians rule!"—*Regis Philbin, talk-show host*

"When I was a kid and the other kids were home watching *Leave It to Beaver*, my father and stepmother were marching me off to the library." —*Oprah Winfrey, talk-show host*

"Being a senior citizen, you can't afford a lot of things, but thanks to my public library, I can read all best-sellers, listen to wonderful music, see movies and operas, read the latest magazines—all for free." —*patron (Milwaukee, Wisconsin)*

"I use my local library as an 'office' when I am conducting a job search." —*patron (Ft. Myers, Florida)*

"My high school library changed my life greatly. Before I came here, the only books I ever read were my schoolbooks . . . Then, one day, I picked out a book. As a result, I found that books ease my mind, along with entertaining me." —*patron (Keansburg, New Jersey)*

"If a disaster struck and I were the only living person left, my main wish would surely be for a standing library." —*patron (North Little Rock, Arkansas)*

Notes

1. Anthony Mullins, "8 Critical Steps to Establish a Customer Service Culture," Ezinearticles, Elite Coaching Alliance, www.ezinearticles.com/?8-Critical-Steps-to-Establish-a-Customer-Service-Culture&id=37272.
2. Robert Spector and Patrick D. McCarthy, *The Nordstrom Way: The Inside Story of America's #1 Customer Service Co.* (New York: Wiley, 1995), 16.
3. Ibid., 35.

4. Greencrest, "Is There a Magic Number?" http://greencrest.com/marketingprose/advertising-frequency-is-there-a-magic-number (April 2006).

5. George Silverman, *The Secrets of Word-of-Mouth Marketing: How to Trigger Exponential Sales through Runaway Word of Mouth* (New York: AMACOM, 2001), 46.

6. Cynthia Henry, "In tight times, N.J. libraries market themselves," *Philadelphia Inquirer,* March 19, 2009, www.philly.com/philly/news/local/41481592.html.

7. ALA Public Information Office files.

When and Where to Buzz

It's easy. Use the three Bs to get the word out: bars, beauty shops, barber shops.

—Liz Cashell, director, Henry County Library, Clinton, Missouri

Libraries have been around a long time and are often taken for granted. People don't talk about what they take for granted. Our challenge is to get their attention and make them *want* to tell others. In other words, we have to give them something to talk about and make it easy, even fun, for them.

If libraries are going to be part of the conversation, we need to be where the conversations are happening. At the Charlotte (Michigan) Community Library, all nineteen staff members are responsible for attending meetings of community groups and feeding back what they hear. They are encouraged to bring all ideas, concerns, and problems to monthly staff meetings, where Director William Siarny says, "No idea or comment is looked down upon."[1]

The Omaha (Nebraska) Public Library has an outreach program called "Have laptop—will travel!" offered in partnership with the Chamber of Commerce (see figure 4.1). Teams of two librarians take the library's message—"We can save you time and money"—to meetings of professional groups and on-site to businesses large and small. Real-estate agencies are a particular focus because of their role in dealing with new residents. Technology librarian Amy Mather said making the library relevant is key to the program's success. Presentations are tailored to each group and address both personal and professional interests. Databases and other online services are demonstrated, and library cards are issued on the spot.

In Wyoming, Isabel Hoy, director of the Goshen County Library, discovered the power of WOMM when she made the rounds of local car-repair shops with an accomplice—the infamous Mudflap Girl (actually a modified version reading a book), who appeared on posters and stickers created as part of a statewide campaign to introduce the newly available Chilton Auto Repair database (see figure 4.2).[2]

"What fun to watch the eyes light up!" Hoy reported. "The guys were initially put in a good mood when they saw Mudflap Girl and more delighted when they saw the wealth of information they could access from their work or home computers. Most of the places had their computers running, so it was easy to do the demonstration. Sometimes there were other customers in the area whom I invited to watch the demonstration. Many of those businesses then bookmarked the access point for Goshen County Library."

The Mudflap Girl campaign got a lot of people talking, and not all of it was favorable. Some—mostly members of the library community—questioned its tastefulness. Tina Lackey, publications and marketing manager for the Wyoming State Library, said the results were worth the controversy. "Most people think it is very funny and understand the irony and humor of the image." Aimed at men who repair their own trucks, the campaign definitely got their attention. The number of searches on the Chilton Auto Repair database quickly

Have laptop—will travel!

Professional librarians can show
your organization how to
• Find quality information
• Save time and money
• Stop wading through google results
• Get what you want

omahapubliclibrary.org

Schedule onsite training today at 444-3399
or email training@omahapubliclibrary.org

Omaha Public Library is offering free business database trainings.

Resources covered:
(all databases can be accessed for free with an Omaha Public Library card)

Business and Company Resource Center - Contains company profiles, brand information, rankings, investment reports, company histories, chronologies and periodicals.

Legal Forms (Nebraska) - Official, State Specific, Federal, Business, Personal, Real Estate and General forms covering hundreds of legal subjects and issues.

Powerfind - Not sure which database to try? Use PowerFind to search up to several databases at the same time.

ProQuest Newsstand - Full text of 300+ U.S. and international news sources. Includes coverage of 150+ major U.S. and international newspapers such as The New York Times, Omaha World-Herald and the Times of London

RefUSA - Source of information on businesses and people for researchers, students and job seekers.

GPO Monthly Catalog – Full-text government publications.

In addition, we will provide a brief overview of the other resources that may be of valuable, including databases for children, young adults, downloadable movies, and host of other products available to you free of charge as an Omaha Public Library card holder.

Contact us today to set up training for your business!

FIGURE 4.1 Omaha (Nebraska) Public Library e-mailed this invitation to local businesses.

Reproduced with permission of the library.

rose to more than 800 a month—not bad for a specialized database in a state with a total population of around 500,000. The campaign also generated considerable humor and a fresh, lighthearted view of libraries. Pickup trucks across Wyoming carried the library's Mudflap Girl stickers. Members of the governor's staff had copies in their offices. The campaign also became the focus of hundreds of blogs, many devoted to marketing and business as well as libraries.

Focusing on the new and unexpected is one of the best ways to get people talking. And when we say new, we mean new to them, not necessarily libraries. Many people, including some who are already library users, still aren't aware of all the services available to them—things like downloadable books and movies, online reserves, gaming, and, of course, databases. We also mean new users, new retirees, new residents, new pet owners—you name it. New moms are said to be the champs of word of mouth, eagerly sharing news about products and services with their friends.[3] People with a new interest tend to be the most interested, most enthusiastic, and most likely to pass along what they learn—in other words, prime targets for WOMM.

Yet another way to join the conversation is to jump in. A great example is the upbeat news release issued by the California State University Library, Fresno, in the wake of US Airways' pilot Chesley B. "Sully" Sullenberger's headline-grabbing landing (see figure 4.3).[4] It sure got us talking!

Another example that got our attention was our copy of *Word of Mouth Marketing: How Smart Companies Get People Talking*, by Andy Sernovitz.[5] It arrived with a message "stamped" on the title page that says, "Tell a Friend! Be Remarkable!" with a URL. Of course, we thought why couldn't libraries do this, and then we learned that a century ago, John Cotton Dana, the library world's first and perhaps greatest promoter, put bookplates in library books with a "tell others" message (see figure 4.4). It's not too late to follow his good example.

Doing the unexpected is another way to get people talking. One of our favorite examples is the "literary speed dating" program "Hardbound to Heartbound" (see figure 4.5) hosted by the Omaha (Nebraska) Public Library. The novelty of this Valentine's Day event, which included a cash bar and door prizes provided by partners, generated considerable newspaper and TV coverage. It also was promoted on the library's Facebook page. People who heard about it are still calling the library, and more events for singles are planned. When asked how they heard about the event, most people (29 percent) said they heard about it from friends or family, followed by the library's website (19 percent) and a variety of other sources (see figure 4.6).

One of our ideas for building a buzz about online services (untried as far as we know) focuses on the message "Did you know you can use the library in your pajamas?" We suggest designating a day or week with prizes to staff and members of the public who wear their pajamas (think photo op). Provide cereal, coffee, and doughnuts—and continuous demonstrations of the library's databases. Be sure to notify the media, and take pictures for the library's newsletter, home page, and blog. If you do it, please let us know.

DELIVERING YOUR MESSAGE

Delivering your message effectively is not just about words. It's also about how you say them. Some people are natural salespeople. They find it easy to engage with people and share their enthusiasm. Fortunately, for the rest of us, there are some simple techniques that can help even shy people become Library Super Salespeople (LSS). In fact, we have had people who attended our workshops say they changed their lives!

Our favorite communication guru, Arch Lustberg, says that if people are going to "buy" your message, they must first trust you; and before they will trust you, they must first like you. Whether they like you depends largely on whether they like how you look. Watch your own reactions to people around you or on TV and see for yourself. Before these people even open their mouths, we are (consciously or not) making judgments about whether we like and trust them. Arch says the simplest and most basic way to get people to like us is to have an open face and body. Simply raising your eyebrows slightly, keeping your shoulders back and your arms and legs apart conveys an openness and approachability that most people will respond to positively. Gesturing with your hands makes you appear more dynamic and adds emphasis to your message. Then think about the opposite—what Arch calls the "closed" position—eyebrows down, arms or legs or both crossed—and what that communicates. Keeping yourself open—physically as well as mentally—during a heated conversation can help to defuse the situation. You will feel better, and so will the other person. Try these postures out with a colleague and see the difference for yourself. Also, feel the difference in the quality of your voice and confidence level.[6]

Most of us naturally have an open face and body when we are relaxed and comfortable. If the conversation starts to get a little tense or you're a bit jittery about trying out WOMM, remember to

FIGURE 4.2
People are talking about the Wyoming Libraries Campaign's Mudflap Girl.

Reproduced with permission of the library.

February 3, 2009

Fresno State library waives fees for hero pilot's missing book

When pilot Chesley B. "Sully" Sullenberger's jetliner wound up in the Hudson River on Jan. 15, so did a book from California State University, Fresno's Henry Madden Library.

Sullenberger's skill in landing his crippled aircraft allowed all 155 people on board to survive. Days after receiving a hero's welcome in his hometown, though, he did what any responsible library patron does: Told the library he didn't have books he borrowed and asked for an extension to get them back or a waiver of overdue or replacement fees.

Fresno State's connection came through an interlibrary loan request that provided the book to a library near Sullenberger's home town of Danville.

Not only will Fresno State forgive the overdue and replacement fees, Library Dean Peter McDonald said he will replace the book and add a bookplate inside the cover dedicating the volume to Sullenberger.

"Here is a national hero you would think would have more important things to worry about," McDonald added. "The world now knows he contacted us almost immediately about the books he'd borrowed that were stuck in the hold of a downed plane. I'd trust my life to a man like Sullenberger. Of course we'll waive the fee."

Sullenberger packed them into his luggage when he took off for the East Coast before the fateful flight. The luggage from Sullenberger's aircraft was collected with other debris as part of the federal investigation of what happened to force the landing on the river between New York City and New Jersey.

FIGURE 4.3   This news release from the California State University, Fresno, made the library the topic of conversation.

Reproduced with permission of the university.

open up. Last but not least, remember to smile. Nothing sells better than a smile.

The beauty of these techniques is that they work in a variety of situations—at a staff or board meeting, media interviews, presentations to groups, parties. The more you practice your open face and body, the easier and more natural it will become both for you to approach other people—and for them to approach you. Most people who work in libraries have big hearts. They believe in what they do and want to make a difference. Sharing that passion with others can be powerful.

There is only one thing more powerful than telling someone your message. That is showing them. The Winnetka-Northfield (Illinois) Public Library District put a laptop computer on the circ desk to make it easy to demonstrate the library's databases. Tailoring the demonstration to the person's interest made this on-the-spot show-and-tell even more powerful. Putting a business card or brochure in the other person's hand also reinforces your message. We highly recommend that libraries print a universal business card (very cheap nowadays) with an attention-getting message that all staff can use. Other types of giveaways—candy, coffee mugs, and calendars—can be great icebreakers. We put these in the "nice but not necessary" category, as there are many less-expensive ways to make your message memorable. Interestingly, one library in the Buzz Project reported that people readily accepted bookmarks, but most refused a mouse pad.

Here are some tips to share with your sales force:

- Be alert for opportunities to do buzz.
- Start with a question: "Have you tried our new . . . ?" or "Do you know about our . . . ?"
- Wear the message. T-shirts, buttons, and other props are great conversation starters.
- Aim every day to surprise and delight library visitors with your customer service skills. Remember things that are routine to you—interlibrary loan, online reserves—may be new to them.
- Make "Tell your friends" your mantra.
- Be especially nice to new users. They are more likely to tell others.
- Don't just tell them. Show them how to use databases or online reserves.
- Put something in their hands—a bookmark, brochure, or business card—to reinforce your message.
- Send a message with your message. Add a signature line on your e-mail.
- Collect testimonials. The next time someone says something nice, get it in writing and ask for permission to quote him or her.
- Share stories about satisfied customers. Everyone loves a success story.
- Set a personal goal for initiating conversations. Raise the bar as your comfort and skill grow.
- Let your passion show! Deliver the message in a way that makes people *feel*—not just *think*—that the library is important.

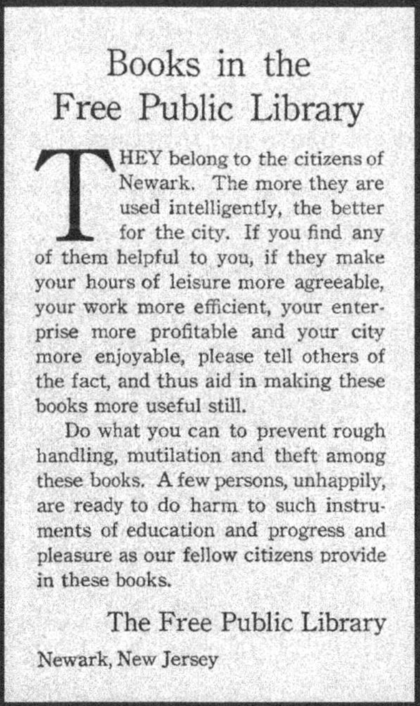

Books in the Free Public Library

THEY belong to the citizens of Newark. The more they are used intelligently, the better for the city. If you find any of them helpful to you, if they make your hours of leisure more agreeable, your work more efficient, your enterprise more profitable and your city more enjoyable, please tell others of the fact, and thus aid in making these books more useful still.

Do what you can to prevent rough handling, mutilation and theft among these books. A few persons, unhappily, are ready to do harm to such instruments of education and progress and pleasure as our fellow citizens provide in these books.

The Free Public Library

Newark, New Jersey

FIGURE 4.4 "Tell your friends"—John Cotton Dana said it first on this bookplate copy.

DEALING WITH THE NEGATIVE

One of the things that people worry about—and will happen—when they are more engaged with the public is having to respond to negative comments or questions. Not just from library users but maybe a friend or neighbor. Is there anyone who hasn't heard, "Gee, is anybody still using the library? I get everything I need online"?

There is only one way to deal with negative comments or questions, and that is *be prepared*. This is especially important if you are introducing a new service or campaign that is potentially controversial, such as fund-raising. Ask your staff what kinds of questions and comments they are hearing and prepare a Q&A sheet with both the easy and tough questions. Make sure everyone on your sales force has a copy. Also make clear they should not attempt to answer questions that they don't understand, are unsure of the answers, or just plain don't feel comfortable answering. Designate someone on the staff or board who is willing and prepared to answer these questions.

Here are some more tips for responding to negatives.

FIGURE 4.5 This "Hardbound to Heartbound" invitation was posted on the Omaha (Nebraska) Public Library's Facebook page.

Reproduced with permission of the library.

- Keep an open face and open body. (It will make you look cool, calm, and collected even if you aren't.)
- Speak simply and sincerely.
- Stay focused on your message.
- Always answer with a positive. Never repeat a negative.
- Keep your answers to the point. If they want to know more, they'll ask.
- Don't let misinformation go uncorrected. If you read something online or hear someone say something about the library that is inaccurate, it is definitely OK to say nicely, but firmly, "Excuse me. I work for the library [serve on the library board], and I think you should know that is not true. The truth is . . ."
- Don't be afraid to say, "I'm sorry, but I don't know." Offer to get back with an answer or refer the person to someone who is prepared and authorized to answer.

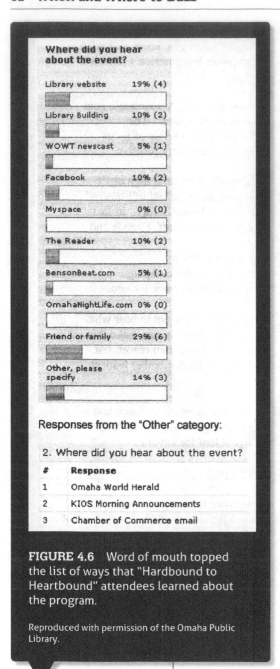

Where did you hear about the event?

Library website — 19% (4)

Library Building — 10% (2)

WOWT newscast — 5% (1)

Facebook — 10% (2)

Myspace — 0% (0)

The Reader — 10% (2)

BensonBeat.com — 5% (1)

OmahaNightLife.com — 0% (0)

Friend or family — 29% (6)

Other, please specify — 14% (3)

Responses from the "Other" category:

2. Where did you hear about the event?

#	Response
1	Omaha World Herald
2	KIOS Morning Announcements
3	Chamber of Commerce email

FIGURE 4.6 Word of mouth topped the list of ways that "Hardbound to Heartbound" attendees learned about the program.

Reproduced with permission of the Omaha Public Library.

Three final words of advice: *Plan. Prepare. Practice.* Anticipate potential negatives and how you will respond. Make sure all members of the library family are prepared and have the support they need. Provide opportunities for them to practice.

E-MEDIA

Face-to-face is still the most powerful form of communication, but online media offer ways to listen and share your message that are easy, fast, and powerful. Web 2.0 is all about engaging in conversations, and word of mouth via e-mail is sometimes referred to as word of mouth on steroids. One click and you can share your opinions (good *and* bad) with an almost infinite number of people. Electronic communication is especially appealing to younger audiences. Participation in the summer reading program sponsored by New York City libraries jumped when teens were allowed to post their book reports online. It's also important to do it right, or you may turn off the tech-savvy people you hope to impress. There are many excellent resources with expert advice on how to use social-networking sites, websites, blogs, wikis, and other new media. We encourage you to learn about and use these tools in addition to, but not instead of, real live conversations.

Some guidelines:

Keep your marketing communication plan handy. Everything you do and say online—whether it's your website, e-newsletter, blog, or Facebook page—should be compatible with the goals, positioning, message, and so forth, outlined in the plan.

Target your e-lists the same way you would target print publications, by audience (parents, businesspeople) or interest (mystery lovers, movie buffs, music fans).

Provide high-quality content. Don't send anything you wouldn't want to receive.

Ask permission before you add someone to an e-list. Always include information on how to unsubscribe.

Be clear about why you are sharing.

Be sure to include a "Share this with a friend" message in your e-newsletter.

Put a "Share this with a friend" link on every web page.

Include surveys and other feedback mechanisms in your e-newsletter and on your website. Be sure to respond.

Pick and choose your e-media. Use online newsletters and e-zines to send news announcements and other timely and useful information. Use blogs to promote a dialogue. They should reflect your personality, philosophy, and perspective.

Reach out and touch someone by text message—especially effective with teens.

Read and follow the guidelines on Facebook and other social-networking sites very carefully.

Keep your e-communications current. Dated information is an even bigger turnoff online.

Don't wait for them to come to you. Provide RSS feeds with new postings of interest on your website or blog.

Educate yourself and others about this new media. Invite input and learn from it.

Give it time. For many people (including library staff), e-media is still a learning experience. Don't be surprised if your audience grows slowly.

ADVOCACY

Advocacy is a prime opportunity to harness the power of WOMM. In advocacy you have a clear target audience—public officials, administrators, other decision makers—and a clear goal—to persuade them to support your cause or point of view, typically to allocate more money.

One of the dangers of advocacy gone awry is that it can sound an awful lot like whining. One of the things we have heard over and over from directors of libraries with strong support is that they don't wait until the annual budget review to make their case. These directors are masters of WOMM who treat other government units as customers. They take them to lunch, invite them to special events, demonstrate new services, send the library's newsletter, recommend books, and suggest other resources. Last, but not least, they ask their advice—and listen. They also engage their trustees and Friends in delivering the library's message to decision makers and the community. We encourage you to follow their good example. ALA and your state library have many excellent resources on advocacy.

SAMPLE Q&A

Q. Haven't computers hurt the library's business?
A. Actually, we're busier than ever! In fact, many people come to the library to use our computers. Students use the computers for research, and many people use them to apply for jobs and fill out tax forms. Books and movies are popular, too!

Q. How can the library afford to buy fancy new checkout machines when you can't afford to be open Fridays and Sundays?
A. We'd love to be open more hours! Unfortunately, all city/county agencies have had to make cuts because of the economy. We were lucky to get a special grant for the checkout machines. Have you tried them yet? They're very easy—and convenient.

Q. Why is it always so noisy in here?
A. I'm sorry if it's too noisy for you. For us, that means business is good! If you need quiet, there's a corner on the second floor reserved for quiet reading. You might also try coming in around 1 o'clock—after story hours and before school lets out.

Q. What's a database?
A. A database is simply an online reference collection—magazines and newspapers, encyclopedias, professional journals, business directories, and many other resources that you can use 24/7. Normally you would have to pay, but you can use them for free on the library's website. Let me show you so you can tell your friends.

Q. I hear the library's going to ask us to pay more taxes. I think it's just fine the way it is.
A. We're glad you like it! We hope to make it even better. Let me give you a copy of this brochure so you can see what we have in mind.

All the tips and strategies in this book apply to advocacy. Here are a few critical ones:

- Prepare a marketing communication plan.
- Craft your message carefully. Focus on community needs and how the library can help address those needs—not what the library needs.
- Take advantage of the connections your trustees and Friends bring.
- Get others to deliver the message for you. Use testimonials.
- Encourage your supporters to tell their friends and to ask their friends to tell their friends.
- Be brief and provide backup materials in writing.
- Listen; don't just talk. Ask their advice.
- Thank them. Send a follow-up.

JUST DO IT

We said WOMM is easy but not necessarily simple. It all comes down to this.

- Get intentional. Have a marketing communication plan.
- Don't settle for good service. Go for great!
- Keep your message simple and consistent.
- Use it consistently in all communications.

THE BUZZ ABOUT BUZZ

Interview with Renee Anderson

Renee Anderson became marketing specialist for the DuPage Library System after the buzz project had started, but she got to see the results.

What do you think was the best thing that came out of the project?
For many libraries, this was their first venture into buzz marketing. The projects encouraged libraries to explore new territory, with fresh knowledge, and a new skill set. These new skills continue to perpetuate.

Our librarians gained confidence and the tools they needed to initiate this "first." Participating library staff also earned the respect and investment of key stakeholders. One of the most important factors involved getting everyone at the library on board and committed to the projects and the ideals the projects represented. Of course, each project achieved results!

Have you observed any changes in how the participating libraries do things?
There was a real emphasis on customer service in the testimonials from participants. There was a realization that these projects, which didn't cost a lot, could change the marketing landscape and perhaps allow for a few extra dollars in future marketing budgets. Especially during these tough economic times, the project served as a reminder that marketing services, improving your image to the community, and promoting your organization might not be too costly.

How would you describe the response after it was completed?
One thing that stood out was how much each library learned in the process. Some libraries held events that were poorly attended, yet knowledge was gained about how to initiate the process and how to reach out to the community. For a few libraries, finding the hours to devote to the project was difficult.

Any other wisdom about word-of-mouth marketing to share?
The buzz marketing projects were amazing. Each project was unique, built self-confidence on the part of the participants, allowed participants to utilize their creative talents, showcased the value of libraries in an extraordinary way, got staff onboard and dedicated to the efforts, built a framework for future projects, and so much more.

When I arrived at DLS, the projects were mostly complete. When I heard the testimonials of those involved, I thought the participants must have had a year to do this fabulous work. When I learned about the short time frame that was involved, I was very impressed.

- Make "Tell your friends" part of the message.
- Give people something to talk about.
- Focus on the new.
- Be relevant.
- Collect and use testimonials when and wherever possible.
- Get the whole library family involved.
- Train and support your staff.
- Look for ways to be part of the conversation.
- Go where the conversations are.
- Listen and feed back what you hear.
- Act on what you hear.
- Stay positive.
- Have fun!

Notes

1. From message to PR Talk e-list, American Library Association, January 27, 2009.
2. Wyoming State Library, The Wyoming Libraries Campaign, http://wyominglibraries .org/campaign.html.
3. "Moms Are Word of Mouth Champions," Biz Report: Viral Marketing (April 22, 2008), www.bizreport.com/2008/04/study_moms_are_word_of_mouth_champions .html.
4. Fresno State University, February 3, 2009, California, www.fresnostatenews .com/2009/02/missingbook.htm.
5. Andy Sernovitz, *Word-of-Mouth Marketing: How Smart Companies Get People Talking,* rev. ed. (New York: Kaplan, 2009).
6. *Controlling the Confrontation: Arch Lustberg on Effective Communication Techniques* (Baltimore: Library Video Network, 1989). Video.

CHAPTER 5

WOMM at Work

Reports from the Front Lines

We encourage you to read these following reports carefully. They are rich with good ideas, strategies, and lessons learned by fifteen pioneering libraries that participated in the Buzz Grant project, sponsored by the DuPage Library System and North Suburban Library System in Illinois.

ADDISON PUBLIC LIBRARY

Good external communication starts with good staff communication.

"I believe in the power of word-of-mouth marketing. Just a question like, 'Do you know about some of the great things that are happening at the library?' can create more interest in programs."

> *I find that when I am enthusiastic and offer something of value—a service or resource folks are unaware of—that the people I talk to become advocates, too.*
>
> —Response to staff survey on word-of-mouth marketing

Introduction

Addison is a landlocked suburb about twenty miles west of Chicago. Although the first settlers arrived in the area in the early 1800s, the community did not begin to grow until the 1950s. There are currently about 36,000 residents. Approximately forty-four languages are spoken in our schools, but the largest ethnic populations are Hispanic and Polish. This project was chosen because the village decided to build a new library using sales-tax monies, and we wanted to get the community involved in and excited about the project. Our ultimate goal was to create support and ownership for our library and a willingness to work for our team.

Goals

- Increase community awareness of the project itself and our need for volunteers to be involved in fund-raising.
- Make staff aware that each transaction with a patron affords an opportunity to increase awareness of the new library and excitement about the things we want to include in this building.
- Get our community excited about the new library.

Objectives

- Get ten new volunteers from our community involved in the fund-raising project.

- Develop partnerships with three community groups that will support our fund-raising efforts.
- Increase questions from our users about the new building by 20 percent.

Key Audiences

- Library "family" (board, staff, advisory committee)
- Library users and supporters
- Key community groups (Women's Club, Rotary, Kiwanis, Lions, local home-owners' associations, Park District seniors)

Message

What's the Buzz? Welcome to a world of possibilities. Help spread the Library's message to the community of Addison.

Strategies

INTERNAL

- Survey staff members to determine their understanding of the library's message and their role in delivering it.
- Track the number of questions asked about the new building to help evaluate how successful we are at getting the word out.
- Hold a luncheon for staff and board members. Provide word-of-mouth marketing tips, copies of the message, and talking points.
- Provide word-of-mouth-marketing training for library department heads.
- Provide new employees with a copy of the talking points, a brochure, and a button to encourage questions.
- Designate a bulletin board in the staff break room for updates about the new building.

EXTERNAL

- Establish Friends of the Addison Public Library and engage them in raising awareness about the new library throughout the community.
- Encourage staff to wear buttons that say "Ask me about YOUR new library!" and to engage library users.
- Make presentations to community groups (e.g., the Kiwanis Club of Addison, the Addison Rotary Club, and the Community Public Relations Group).

Tools

- Staff surveys
- Buttons for staff
- Brochure about new building using the key message and talking points
- Form for staff to complete whenever they hear positive comments about the library

Addison Public Library
Four Friendship Plaza
June 2008

What's the Buzz?
Welcome to a world of possibilities.

Help spread the Library's message to the community of Addison.

FIGURE 5.1 The Addison (Illinois) Public Library published this brochure with its message and a Q&A about its building project for staff.

Budget

Less than $100 for buttons. Brochures and other materials were printed in-house.

Impact

Developing a way to communicate with all staff members, especially those who do not have immediate access to e-mail, was one of the most successful aspects of this project. Staff willingly began wearing the "Ask me about YOUR new library!" buttons and engaged in conversations about our new building. We had 413 questions about the new building in the first three months of the project. Staff surveys were distributed before and after the project. Thirty-one of forty-one indicated they felt more comfortable delivering the library message.

The Friends of the Library are now an established group supporting the library in many ways. Although the group was not a direct result of the word-of-mouth-marketing project, using these techniques will increase, and hopefully sustain, membership levels. A number of fund-raising projects have begun. More of the community seems aware of the building project than when we began.

Lessons Learned

Library staff members need to know the role each plays in developing and sustaining the image of the library in the community. When each of us interacts with someone, whether in the building or at the grocery store, we convey a message about the library. We want that message to be positive. This is a difficult concept to promote, especially to staff members who do not live in the community. It is something we need to remind the staff about frequently.

With the opening of a beautiful new library, it is really easy to be positive about all the great things we have in this building for our users. All of the staff seem very proud of this new home and are willing to help patrons find their way around the building and to answer questions. The community response has been overwhelmingly positive.

Getting all of our staff members to realize that they contribute to the word-of-mouth network even if they do not live in Addison is a challenge. Sometimes it's difficult to remember that each of us is an ambassador for libraries wherever we go.

I believe in the power of word-of-mouth marketing. Just a question like "Do you know about some the great things that are happening at the library?" can create more interest in programs.

I am working on a new campaign to increase attendance at our library programs for adults. I plan to send information to each staff member in the Adult Services and Circulation departments and ask them to talk with patrons whenever possible.

—*Sally Schuster, Public Relations Coordinator (schuster@addisonlibrary.org)*

BARTLETT PUBLIC LIBRARY DISTRICT

Customer comments jumped 600 percent with 80 percent positive as a result of this library's focus on improving customer service and internal communication.

"Informed and knowledgeable staff members are better able to provide good customer service."

Introduction

Bartlett Public Library District is located in the village of Bartlett, a western suburb of Chicago. The town has seen a large growth in population and is expected to peak at around 45,000. Many residents commute to the city for their jobs. Currently, the library district has a population of 36,000. About 80 percent are Caucasian, 10 percent are Asian, and the rest are a mix of Hispanic and African American. Many people use the library and attend our programs and check out materials. We want all library experiences to be positive and decided to focus on building better communication and understanding among staff. Better internal service will translate into better patron services. When people talk about the library, we want it to always be in positive terms.

Goals

- Have the community rediscover the library and make the library part of their everyday lives.
- Create library advocates in the community through positive experiences at the library.
- Develop a staff attitude of "X-treme Customer Service."
- Develop respect and good service between departments as they work toward our common goal.

Objectives

- Promote an attitude of service that is customer—not task—driven.
- Increase customer feedback through comment cards by 20 percent so that we can better respond to their needs and wants.
- Increase the number of positive comments from customers.

Key Audiences

- Staff
- Library users

Message

We Make It Happen!

Strategies

INTERNAL
- Conduct three staff surveys: (1) self-evaluation of customer service behaviors, (2) internal customer survey, and (3) word-of-mouth marketing.

- Hold an in-service day for staff and library board members to introduce word-of-mouth marketing, the role of staff, and its impact. Provide fun gifts such as wax lips and stress balls.
- Develop message with members of the management team.
- Develop a pocket-sized "Best Practices" brochure. Provide copies to all current and new staff.
- Distribute a small item each week to staff in their in-boxes both as a reward and a reminder of our "Best Practices" and customer-driven service.
- Issue e-mails every Monday about what is happening at the library that week.
- Publish a "What's Happening This Week" calendar, available on all desktops in the building.
- Put the library newsletter in all staff in-boxes and all service points.
- Feature information on customer service and word-of-mouth marketing in the staff newsletter.
- Broadcast e-mails to all staff featuring reminders of customer service points as well as positive comments received on the new comment forms.
- Encourage staff to check their e-mails, in-boxes, and department boards each shift for any information that may be posted or distributed.

EXTERNAL
- Encourage staff to ask patrons to fill out comment forms when they have concerns or praise for the library.
- Provide Bartlett Library business cards to all staff to use when they are out in the community.

Tools

- New "Tell Us—We're Listening!" comment forms with a check-off box asking for permission to use comments in publicity.
- New customer comment boxes and forms for each department.
- A pocket-sized "Best Practices" brochure on exceptional customer service with our message "We Make It Happen!" This was developed by a team of managers and introduced at a staff meeting. It describes the expected behavior of employees and empowers them to handle situations and to make reasonable exceptions to policies and procedures.
- Trinkets and rewards for staff. These included a compass key ring with the message, "Bartlett Library, on the trail to achieving great customer service." A deck of cards that said, "Deal fairly. Listen, respond calmly and solve the problem." A clown nose and the reminder to "Bring a positive attitude and have fun."
- Bulletin boards were hung in all departments and the staff lounge for quick and easy communication.

Budget

$900, including food for in-service day, giveaways, and bulletin boards

Impact

All in all, I am very happy with the results and the ongoing effort. Since implementation of our new comment boxes and forms, we went from 2 comments per month to an average of 13.6 comments per month. Eighty percent of the comments were positive. The other 20 percent had recommendation for improvements. These are very helpful in our efforts to provide complete customer satisfaction.

One of the most successful aspects of this project is increased communication between departments. Informed and knowledgeable staff members are better able to provide good customer service. Staff are learning about the roles of the various positions in the library. They also are more aware of what is going on in the building.

One of the least successful aspects is keeping the staff motivated and aware at all times. A month after distributing the "Best Practices" brochure, staff were queried at a staff meeting, and only a few could identify the ten actions listed.

Overall, there has been an improvement in communication that has resulted in better customer service and public awareness. We have continued to use and increase our internal communication efforts.

- The "Best Practices" trifold is given to every new employee, and additional copies are always available in the staff lounge.
- All staff newsletters include something about customer service practices. A new feature titled "A Day in the Life of . . ." showcases different staff members and their daily duties.
- The library has increased its presence at many community events (Movies in the Park, National Night Out, Health Fair, a professional float in the Independence Day Parade); hosted a Chamber After Hours event with more than 100 chamber members in attendance; and added more visits to senior venues.
- Participation in chamber events resulted in a library staff member receiving the Business Person of the Year Award from the Bartlett Chamber of Commerce.
- The library director was featured in local newspaper as one of the top five people to watch in 2009.
- We held mandatory staff meetings to review our updated Personnel Policy and Procedures Manual.
- The staff-room bulletin board always has something posted: important information about programs/services; customer service tips and suggestions; comments from our "Tell Us—We're Listening!" forms; dates to remember; and so forth.

Lessons Learned

We did a general survey to the public asking them how they learn about library programs and services. The majority response was that they learned about the library services and programs from library staff or neighbors and friends. This demonstrates the power of word-of-mouth marketing in the community. Out of fifty-six surveys received, thirty-five responses cited staff or word of mouth.

Results from staff surveys demonstrated a need for improved internal communication in the library. Many ideas have been generated from the responses. Twenty-eight staff members (62 percent) responded to a follow-up survey of five questions asking about word of mouth and external and internal customer service. Overall, people were more aware of what is going on in the library (better communication) and perceived an improvement in external and internal customer service.

—Susan Westgate, Assistant Director (swestgate@barlett.lib.il.us)

BEACH PARK COMMUNITY CONSOLIDATED SCHOOL DISTRICT 3 (BEACH PARK MIDDLE SCHOOL)

Being consistent—and persistent—paid off for this library media center.

"One teacher flat-out told me that it was because of my personal reminder that he came. He had seen the e-mail but had quickly forgotten it. Repetition helps."

Introduction

Beach Park Middle School is located in the far northeastern region of Illinois. Our students come from a wide economic background and share their many diverse cultures. There are more than 1,000 students in the building, mostly sixth to eighth grades. Our library also serves a pre-K to eighth-grade school-within-a-school whose students have special needs. There is one certified librarian for five different schools, and we are working hard to improve students' test scores.

Over the past few years, the library has received grants to purchase replicas, realia, costumes, and manipulatives to help children use all of their senses in learning. Cataloging, sorting, storing, and promoting these items have been a challenge. The library is working on cooperatively teaching with educators so the unique items are utilized.

Goals

- Teachers will understand that collaborating with the librarian will add depth to their teaching.
- Teachers will know about the "hidden gems" our collection contains.

Objectives

- Recruit two advocates at each school to share something about one of our seven district libraries or the librarian every week.
- Co-teach with one teacher at each school who I have not co-taught with before by the end of the school year.

Key Audience

Teachers

Message

The library and you: partners in learning

Strategies

- Invite two people from each school to be advocates. We asked them to tell two colleagues something about one of the school libraries, the professional library, or the librarian at least once a week.
- Establish a "Did you know . . . ?" short e-mail for announcements of special interest.
- Publish an all-staff weekly article on programs, services, and happenings for the different libraries.

- Check in with teachers to see if the library can help them during School Improvement Days.
- Perform "Roving Reference" by stopping by classrooms during breaks and before or after school to offer assistance.
- Eat lunch with teachers to make the librarian accessible.
- Promote the professional library by offering study groups about new collections. Provide refreshments.
- Monitor grant e-lists and pass on opportunities to collaborate with other teachers.
- Demonstrate responsiveness by following up within one day of receiving requests or questions.

Budget

Only my time

Impact

Most successful: the fact that teachers in other schools are asking me to come to their classroom to share our "gems." Teachers are also realizing that if you take a little time to work with the certified librarian, students will benefit from the collaboration.

We greatly increased the amount of materials we loan between schools. Last year it was 5; this year it was more than 300. Our interlibrary loans to district libraries also increased from 10 to more than 150. The carts of books that we pull for teachers on topics increased from 40 to 80. These are measurable indicators that teachers are beginning to find and use some of our "hidden gems."

Least successful: the lack of training and follow-through for the advocates. I was able to obtain at least one advocate for all but one school. Of these eleven advocates, one will not be returning next year. I plan on strengthening this "Friends" group by offering more training, food, and occasional meetings.

I did co-teach with many more teachers than I have in the past. I am also working with eighteen new teachers to consider how we might work together.

I particularly used word-of-mouth strategies to promote a grant study group. The first time we offered this, no one came. For this one, we put out a "Did you know . . . ?" e-mail. During a School Improvement Day, we wandered around the cafeteria while people were snacking before the meeting and personally invited them. This time we had six people show and another four who couldn't make the meeting but did want the handouts and information. One teacher flat-out told me that it was because of my personal reminder that he came. He had seen the e-mail but quickly forgotten it. Repetition helps.

I continued the "Roving Reference" as a mainstay of what I do. The more I know what is going on in the classroom, the more I can offer suggestions and collaborate with teachers.

Lessons Learned

Developing positive relationships with teachers will encourage them to utilize the wide variety of library resources. Teachers often do not have time to make formal requests, come down, or do an in-depth search of the catalog. The easier you can make it for them, the more the library resources will be used. If it means I need to walk a cart of resources to a teacher in order for them to be used, I'll do it.

Every person who enters the library is a chance to build your grassroots support. Did they encounter someone friendly? Did they feel welcome? Did they have their needs met? Do they know what your ten-second message, your thirty-second message, or your two-minute message is?

I am finding that if I bring a really great program or surprise a person with the speed of my response, he or she will often comment on it to other people. We have begun reporting monthly to the school board, so they are now aware of the time spent in other buildings, programs held, and collaborative projects with teachers.

—*Jeanné Lohfink, District Librarian (jlohfink@bpd3.org)*

BP INFORMATION SERVICES (NAPERVILLE)

They listened! A primary strategy for this special library was a survey of users. Although they expected to get twenty-five returned, they received more than one hundred.

"We actually had stories where people said we saved them money, and that was just gold."

Introduction

The BP Library serves the information needs of BP employees and contractors worldwide by offering specialized news, business and technical bulletins, more than seventy-five information databases, personalized reference, and other library services. Users include petroleum engineers, research chemists, commodity traders, market managers, and communication professionals. Although our physical library is in Naperville, most customers use our intranet-based services. We lack a good handle on who our users are because most never walk into the library. We are a small group—five full-time and three part-time staff members—with a potential clientele of more than 100,000 worldwide.

Goals

- Increase awareness of our services by getting to know our customers and their needs better.
- Better target new resources to a globally dispersed user base.

Objectives

- Collect feedback from at least twenty-five employees to use in rebranding the library.
- Educate staff about word-of-mouth marketing and their role.

Key Audiences

- Staff—full- and part-time
- BP employees, starting with our current users and new website visitors

Message

You Have Questions—We Have Answers. Just Ask Us!

Strategies

- Develop and conduct an online survey of our users. We promoted participation by running a banner across the top of several of our website pages.
- Make better use of our message (slogan). We attached the slogan to all our internal e-mail signatures and as a header on our new intranet site.
- Create an e-mail signature with a link to the survey.
- Dedicate one monthly staff meeting to word-of-mouth marketing. We covered the basics and solicited ideas from all staff members.
- Coach staff on setting up personal e-mail signatures.
- Have staff identify their best customers and methods for reaching them with the survey request.
- Include the link in various current-awareness and newsletter products.
- Hold a prize drawing for those who participated in the survey.

Tools

- Online survey—we purchased an upgraded Survey Monkey membership.
- Spiffy and low-cost business cards.
- Amazon gift certificates for the survey prize drawing: four $25 prizes and one $100 grand prize.

Budget

$400 for the Survey Monkey membership, printing, and prizes

Impact

We now see more opportunities than obstacles because we know our users are on our side. Much to our surprise, 130 customers completed the survey. Almost half the respondents offered specific comments and testimonials. We actually had stories where people said we saved them money, and that was just gold. It made us review our services and think about how we were reaching our patrons. We hadn't taken the time to review the whole picture before.

Other impacts: we saw a spike in website use that may have resulted from our efforts to "talk up" the survey but have no way of verifying that. We feel we now have a pool of volunteers we can tap to do usability testing of our website during the upgrade. We also experienced renewed sensitivity to libraryspeak that will be incorporated in the updating of our intranet website and rebranding effort.

We plan on using surveys again, for feedback on the updated website and its usability. We are engaging our survey participants in other efforts to market our services and resources. They have helped us gauge interest in some new projects and were active during product trials. This group is a real asset for us.

We will ask for testimonials and direct feedback about our services when we launch our new internal website.

Lessons Learned

- Involve the whole staff at every stage. Sharing enthusiasm was contagious to the rest of the staff.

- Respect the customer. Keep the survey short. Offer a prize. Test the survey with a pilot group first.
- Listen to the customer. Responses showed that some customers didn't understand the library jargon we use.
- Ask for stories and specifics. Good customer stories and testimonials boost staff morale and can be used elsewhere in our marketing plan.
- Look for gaps. Respondents expressed a lack of knowledge of some of our services—ones we thought they knew about.
- Partner with customers. More than 60 percent of our current users found us by referral, so word of mouth is already working for us.
- Prepare for change. This project invigorated our staff. We now see more opportunities than obstacles because we know our users are on our side.

—Joyce Fedeczko, Information Services Director (joyce.fedeczko@bp.com) and Nancy Maloney, Electronic Resources Librarian (nancy.maloney@bp.com)

COOK MEMORIAL PUBLIC LIBRARY DISTRICT

This library harnessed word-of-mouth marketing using a 1920s theme to get people talking.

"One of the keys to word-of-mouth marketing is feeling like you have a little bit of extra knowledge about something. It surprised me how little things, like sending e-mail updates, really kept our group motivated and feeling 'in the know.'"

Introduction

The Cook Memorial Public Library District serves 60,000 residents in six towns: Libertyville, Vernon Hills, Mettawa, Mundelein, Green Oaks, Indian Creek, and unincorporated Libertyville Township. The suburban district is thirty miles north of Chicago. The Big Read is a community-wide reading campaign that focused on two books—*The Great Gatsby* (for adults) and *Dave at Night* (for youth). Because the district encompasses portions of six towns, we wanted to unite the community as one library district. The Cook Memorial Public Library District partnered with schools, cultural centers, and community organizations.

Goal

Create a buzz about our Big Read program.

Objectives

- Enhance staff knowledge of The Big Read by 100 percent.
- Develop a core of 50 "Big Read Community Spokespeople."
- Increase participation in The Big Read by doubling attendance and circulating 150 copies of Big Read books.

Key Audiences

- Library staff, board, Friends
- The public: regular patrons and nonusers

- Students and school faculty
- Local businesses
- Community leaders

Message

The Big Read—What Page Are You On?

Strategies

INTERNAL

- Host a staff Lunch and Learn program on word-of-mouth marketing.
- Hold a staff party to kick off The Big Read. Our party had a speakeasy theme, complete with "bathtub ginger ale," a password-protected entrance, and a "police raid."
- Send weekly activity e-mails to staff so they know exactly what is going on.
- Ask staff members to help distribute event guides for The Big Read by dropping them off at places in the community they frequent. Every time they took twenty fliers to distribute, they earned a chance for a $20 restaurant gift certificate.
- Provide buttons and 1920s headgear for staff to wear as conversation starters.

EXTERNAL

- Identify key communicators and encourage them to spread the word about The Big Read. Invite them to pose for READ posters, holding the featured books.
- Collect testimonials and photos from key communicators about their favorite memory of *The Great Gatsby* or *Dave at Night.*
- Publish a special edition of our e-newsletter to highlight The Big Read activities.
- Ask schools to pass out an event brochure or read an events announcement each day or both.
- Partner with Main Street Libertyville (the downtown organization that plans special events) to incorporate our 1920s theme into their Girls Just Wanna Have Fun weekend. The weekend was scheduled during the second weekend of The Big Read promotion. Our graphic designer created marketing collateral for the weekend showing girls having fun in 1920s garb. Sixteen ads for the weekend, including a tagline about The Big Read, were placed in three local papers over a three-week span.
- Invite other local businesses and media to partner with the library and support The Big Read by distributing event brochures and hanging READ posters.
- Send information about The Big Read to press contacts, with a focus on the new and the unusual.
- Include the "Tell your friends" tagline on publicity materials.
- Provide a What Page Are You On? ad to be shown on sixteen movie theater screens daily for six weeks.

Tools

- What Page Are You On? buttons
- Feather headbands or gangster hats for staff to wear the week of the kickoff

- Special web pages for both books
- E-mail newsletters
- Posters for schools, local businesses, and the library
- Partner organizations
- Testimonials for website

Budget

The project was part of a grant the library district received from the National Endowment for the Arts (NEA). The NEA matched $6,000 of our budget, giving us a total of $12,000 to spend on the project. The budget included buying books, purchasing advertising and other publicity costs, and hosting thirty programs.

Impact

- One hundred staff members attended trainings and motivation events.
- Sixty-two staff members passed out events brochures to local businesses.
- Everyone on staff received weekly updates via e-mail, and printed copies were placed in staff areas.
- More than fifty community leaders received information about The Big Read and agreed to pose for READ posters; seventy-five copies were distributed in the community.
- Ten people provided testimonials.
- The Big Read books circulated 693 times—400 percent higher than our goal of 150.
- Attendance goals were doubled. During the month of April, we saw a 10 percent increase in program attendees who said they found out about a library program from "word of mouth."
- Many staff members said they wore the What Page Are You On? buttons on their purses and coats and got involved in conversations about the book all over town. One got caught talking about the book in the checkout line at the grocery store!

Lessons Learned

One of the keys to word-of-mouth marketing is feeling like you have a little bit of extra knowledge about something. It surprised me how little things, like sending e-mail updates, really kept our group motivated and feeling "in the know."

With more than thirty programs in thirty days, we found that publicizing all these events was overwhelming. We met our attendance goals but had hoped to exceed them.

—*Erin Maassen, Public Relations Manager (emaassen@cooklib.org)*

CRYSTAL LAKE PUBLIC LIBRARY

A clever name and logo—Project Shoehorn—helped capture the public's attention.

"We felt that word-of-mouth marketing was a successful way of communicating during Project Shoehorn. The average person knew the name and concept through a clear and succinct message about our library and services."

FIGURE 5.2 The Crystal Lake (Illinois) Public Library used this logo for its Project Shoehorn.

Reproduced with permission of the library.

Introduction

Established in 1913, the Crystal Lake Public Library (CLPL) was rated one of the nation's top ten libraries by Hennen's American Public Library Ratings in 1999 and 2008 in the 25,000–49,000 population category. It serves a city population of 39,788 plus an unincorporated area.

Following a failed 2004 referendum for a new building, CLPL undertook a major reorganization as a short-term solution to our space limitations. It was estimated that this effort would allow us five to eight more years in the current building without major expansion.

Our concern was that our public would perceive the reorganization work on the library as a long-term solution to our space needs instead of a short-term solution. In spite of our best efforts, our public has many misconceptions about when the library was last expanded, how it was financed, and why we need a larger library.

This campaign was intended to create excitement about the work completed on the building while reminding our patrons that it was not a long-term solution.

Goals

- Remind our patrons and the public that the library is a valuable community asset.
- Keep the library at the forefront of the public's mind when it comes to informational and recreational interests and needs.
- Increase the community's understanding of the library's continued space needs.
- Increase the community's understanding of how the library can better serve their needs with more space.

Objectives

- Staff and board members will feel comfortable delivering our message to our key audiences.
- Thirty community leaders and thirty patrons will take library tours.
- One thousand people will attend our Grand Reopening Weekend.
- Two thousand key message handouts will be distributed.
- Build a core of fifty library champions.

Key Audiences

- Staff and board members
- Library users
- Community leaders

Message

Since 1913 we've been growing with our community. Though challenged by space limitations, our remodeling aims to provide you with the best possible library service.

Strategies

INTERNAL

- Survey staff and board to gauge their comfort level with word-of-mouth marketing.
- Provide educational materials and presentations to staff and board to increase their comfort level with word-of-mouth marketing.
- Provide Project Shoehorn shirts for staff and board. Staff was allowed to wear jeans to work on days they wore their Project Shoehorn shirts as an incentive to communicate about the project.

EXTERNAL

- Create a logo and tagline for the campaign, to be used on handouts, newsletters, shirts, and signage.
- Send a personal letter to potential library champions, explaining the goals of our campaign and our challenges and inviting them to become part of the solution.
- Devote space in our newsletter and on our website to our key message, including relevant news and information.
- Send press releases, not only to the newspapers, but also to the City Council, Chamber of Commerce, Downtown Association, and Friends of the Library.
- Invite the mayor and two state legislators to speak at our Grand Reopening. Provide them with information ahead of time about our project, our message, and our goals. Ask them to help deliver our message in the community.
- Send special invitations to our Grand Reopening, including an invitation to tour the library, to key officials and supporters, including the mayor, our senator and representative, members of the City Council, Friends of the Library, our architect and construction manager, the Chamber of Commerce board, and library donors.
- Use the time during the tours to deliver our message.

Tools

- Handouts with the key message and talking points for staff, board members, and CLPL champions
- Shirts with the logo and message for staff and board

Budget

$2,000, including shirts for staff and board and in-house printing

Impact

- More than 1,000 people attended our Grand Reopening weekend.
- More than 6,000 key message handouts were distributed.
- The mayor, City Council, and a number of local legislators, as well as Friends and foundation members, took a special tour during our Grand Reopening weekend. We also had more than 70 members of the public tour the library.

One of the most surprising outcomes was the number of people in the public who knew about Project Shoehorn and talked about it. We overheard people at public events, even kids at school, mentioning Project Shoehorn by name.

When seeking sponsors for our summer reading program, we were amazed at the number of people who mentioned Project Shoehorn and asked about our progress.

We heard stories that people were discussing Project Shoehorn on the commuter train. The most compelling story that we heard was from a patron who found himself seated on a plane next to someone who, upon hearing that the man lived in Crystal Lake, asked about Project Shoehorn. It turns out that the other passenger had heard about Crystal Lake's renovation project through the "grapevine."

Through staff and board follow-up surveys, we determined that they felt comfortable delivering our message. We found that our patrons were naturally curious about what was happening at the library, and our Project Shoehorn shirts inspired many comments and questions about what was going on, making it easy to transition to our message.

Lessons Learned

Your message needs to be brief and easy to remember. We felt that word-of-mouth marketing was a successful way of communicating during Project Shoehorn. The average person knew the name and concept through a clear and succinct message about our library and services. We plan to use these techniques in future communication initiatives.

—*Kathryn I. Martens, Library Director (kmartens@CrystalLakeLibrary.org)*

GLEN ELLYN PUBLIC LIBRARY

Database use skyrocketed when this library staff got talking.

"This project opened my eyes to an entirely new way of marketing. I realized that you don't need a lot of money for promotion—creativity and passion can go a long way."

Introduction

The Glen Ellyn Public Library is a suburban library serving a population of about 27,000. We wanted to do a better job of marketing our library without spending a lot. Although circulation is good (571,000 in the last year), the library's databases are not used much. We decided to focus on NoveList because we felt it was particularly underused by both patrons and staff. Readers' advisory is an area where staff members often lack confidence, and NoveList can be a big help. This is a great tool when somebody says, "I like to read Amy Tan. What else can I read?"

Goal

Glen Ellyn readers will be aware of and use the NoveList database to help them find good books.

Objectives

- Increase use of NoveList by 10 percent.
- Show ten patrons each week how to use NoveList.
- Collect fifteen testimonials for use in future NoveList promotions.

Key Audiences

- Staff
- Library users in search of good books to read

Message

Try NoveList!
- NoveList can help you can find books to fit your individual taste.
- NoveList covers fiction titles for all age groups.
- We will be happy to show you how to use NoveList.
- You can access NoveList 24/7 from your home computer.
- We have a computer class on how to use NoveList.

Strategies

- Provide hands-on training to all staff members on how to use NoveList.
- Conduct one-on-one demonstrations of NoveList at the Adult Services desk.
- Conduct weekly quiz with staff using NoveList to find answers.

Tools

- A colorful information packet titled "The Buzz is about NOVELIST" was given to all staff. The packet included the project's background and goals, facts about buzz marketing, key messages, and talking points.
- Bookmarks promoting NoveList for various age groups—young adults, parents, book-discussion groups, pleasure readers
- Restaurant certificates for prizes to staff

Budget

$75, including three $15 gift cards, printing, and miscellaneous supplies

Impact

NoveList sessions rose from 52 in June 2006 to 141 in June 2007 and 194 in July 2007—a 375 percent increase! Most of our customers were completely unfamiliar with the database and were thrilled to learn about it. Forty-five demonstrations were conducted over eight weeks. These were very effective, and patrons appreciated the hands-on training. Parents were particularly pleased that they could find books geared for their children's reading levels.

Staff loved the weekly quiz. It really helped motivate them to become adept at using NoveList, which translated to becoming more confident in demonstrating it to patrons. They told me that they were unaware of some of the great things that it could do, and practicing searches taught them a lot about the product.

A major outcome is that staff members better understand how important the personal one-on-one contact is. Talking to patrons goes a long way because those patrons will tell their friends about what they learned.

This project opened my eyes to an entirely new way of marketing. I realized that you don't need a lot of money for promotion—creativity and passion can go a long way.

Lessons Learned

In hindsight, I should have emphasized the testimonial part of the project more. Even though I know that patrons who were shown how to use NoveList liked the product, staff didn't write down what they said.

I learned that word-of-mouth marketing is fun and really taps into your creative side. Enthusiasm and resourcefulness go a long way in promoting a product or service. The project inspired me to look at marketing from many angles and realize that it's not necessarily how much you spend. With some imagination, your budget doesn't have to define your success.

—*Ann McDonald, Marketing Associate (amcdonald@gepl.org)*

HIGHLAND PARK PUBLIC LIBRARY

This library doubled subscriptions to its e-newsletter using good old-fashioned word of mouth.

"Involving the circulation staff in subscribing patrons to the e-newsletter will be an ongoing initiative."

Introduction

The Highland Park Public Library serves a suburban community of 31,365 residents. Our location, in a park setting in downtown Highland Park, makes it readily accessible to residents and businesses. In early 2007, the library introduced a monthly electronic newsletter (e-newsletter) as a way to improve communication about library programs and services. The Buzz Grant provided an opportunity to use word-of-mouth marketing as a means to introduce the community to the library's e-newsletter and to increase its subscriber base.

Goals

- Create awareness of and interest in the library's e-newsletter and encourage people to subscribe to the e-newsletter.
- Encourage patrons to feel that by subscribing to the e-newsletter they would have access to the "inside track" of what is going on at the library and "buzz" about what they learned.
- Increase attendance at library programs and use of services that are promoted in the e-newsletter.

Objectives

- Increase subscribers from 300 to 1,000 by the end of the two-month word-of-mouth campaign.
- Achieve an open rate of 80 percent among those receiving the e-newsletter.
- Enable staff to feel more confident in delivering the library's message.

Key Audiences

- Staff
- Library users
- Others interested in the library

Message

"Extra! Extra! E All About It!"

Strategies

INTERNAL

- Form a word-of-mouth marketing committee.
- Present word-of-mouth-marketing tips and e-newsletter campaign at all staff meetings.
- Provide a one-page tip sheet for staff with important information about the e-newsletter and how patrons can subscribe.
- Provide stickers with teaser message ("Extra! Extra! E All About It!") for staff to wear.
- Recruit Friends of the Library to staff the campaign kiosk and buzz about the campaign.
- Provide a "Kickoff" cake for staff to celebrate the campaign launch.

EXTERNAL

- Display "Extra! Extra!" message on bookmarks, tent cards for tables, and banners for desks in Adult Services and Youth departments to create interest and excitement.
- Place a "pop-up" kiosk for subscribing to the e-newsletter in the lobby. Use balloons and signage to help draw attention. Display the e-newsletter's sign-up form on two computers.
- Create a buzz at the local train station with two library staff members dressed as newsboys handing out sample e-newsletters and sign-up information during morning rush hour. The staff wore newsboy aprons with the "Extra! Extra! E All About It!" message.
- Distribute candy with the library's URL to remind people they could sign up from home.
- Make a presentation at a community-wide meeting attended by members of the City Council, civic and community organizations, and the local school system.
- Encourage those attending library programs to subscribe.

Tools

- "Kickoff" cake and stickers for staff
- Bookmarks
- Tent cards for table tops
- Banners for desks
- Helium balloons in the library's colors (orange and green) with the letter E (these were placed around the library to attract attention)
- Candy with the library's URL printed on the wrapper

Budget

$285 for balloons, custom-ordered candy with the library's URL, aprons for the "newsboys," and a "Kickoff" cake to motivate and excite the staff for the launch of the word-of-mouth campaign

Impact

During the two-month campaign, subscriptions to the e-newsletter increased by 125, from 300 to 425, plus another 100 people subscribed to the e-newsletter but had not yet confirmed their subscriptions. (This step has since been dropped.)

We feel that we did a credible job of creating awareness about the e-newsletter. Converting people to become subscribers, however, was another matter. When this project began, 300 people had already subscribed. To attract additional subscribers, it was necessary to reach another tier of library patrons as the frequent library users had perhaps already subscribed.

Additionally, we found that some people did not understand the difference between e-mail notification, which many patrons receive, and the e-newsletter. Many patrons did not realize that these are two different library communications. This confusion may have contributed to a hesitation to subscribe to the e-newsletter.

We may have benefited from including more staff incentives to encourage staff to "buzz" about the e-newsletter. Perhaps offering an incentive for every three to five people that staff signed up would have increased our subscriber base.

To encourage more patrons to subscribe to the e-newsletter, circulation staff now ask those applying for new library cards if they would like to subscribe. This extra effort has helped to increase subscriptions to more than 1,000. As we are seeing, when the circulation staff "buzz" about the e-newsletter and offer to subscribe patrons on the spot, the number of subscribers increases.

The communications company that manages the e-newsletter mailing has reported that the average open rate of e-newsletters for their clients is 20 to 30 percent. The overall open rate for our e-newsletter is 50 percent, well above the average quoted. Given the average open rate, aiming for an open rate of 80 percent may have been unrealistic.

Lessons Learned

Building the subscriber base of the e-newsletter continues to be important for the library. Involving the circulation staff in subscribing patrons to the e-newsletter will be an ongoing initiative as this has proven successful. We will continue to have staff promote the e-newsletter during conversations with patrons and will continue to promote the e-newsletter to program attendees and at community meetings.

We also hope that the e-newsletter content will generate its own buzz as it features advance notice of special events, giveaways, lists of recommended and new books, and lists of what the movers and shakers in the community are reading. It is our hope that by including interesting and special content in the e-newsletter, the open rate will continue to be high and may even reach that elusive 80 percent.

—Beth Keller, Marketing Specialist (bkeller@hplibrary.org)

MOUNT PROSPECT PUBLIC LIBRARY

Online program registration tripled when staff started spreading the word.

"Word-of-mouth marketing was a very effective tool for communicating this message. The price was right, and we proved that talking with users worked better than distributing fliers."

Introduction

This suburban community, located about twenty miles northwest of Chicago, was voted the "Best Place to Raise Kids in the United States" in 2008 by *Business Week.* This award reflects the fact that Mount Prospect offers affordable housing for middle-income families, an excellent school system, and a host of amenities. The library is one of the amenities that helped our village win this title. Mount Prospect was also recognized for its diverse population.

In February 2007, the library introduced a redesigned website. We decided to promote online registration for programs for two reasons: to encourage patrons to interact with the website and to make them aware that they could register for programs directly. Prior to this promotion, patrons who asked about a library program were directed to the registration desk to sign up, and the staff would manage the process. We wanted to let patrons know that they could handle this process themselves from home.

Goals

- Promote online program registration to patrons within the library and out in the community.
- Gain experience with word-of-mouth marketing.

Objective

Increase use of online registration to 25 percent of all program registrations.

Key Audiences

- Staff
- Library users

Message

Did you know? It's easy to sign up online for a library program.

Strategies

INTERNAL
- Measure staff's comfort level with word-of-mouth marketing through pre- and postcampaign staff surveys.
- Organize a staff training session led by the consultants. (This session covered buzz marketing as well as details of our message.)
- Instruct staff at department meetings on how to demonstrate online registration to patrons.
- Train library board members on how to talk about and demonstrate online registration.
- Establish secret "listeners" to reward staff members with cookies when they are overheard promoting online registration to patrons.
- Develop a staff contest rewarding staff members who demonstrate online registration with gift certificates to local businesses. Every time a staff member demonstrates online registration, he or she completes and submits an entry form for a raffle.
- Kick off the campaign by providing staff with giant cookies featuring the campaign message.
- Encourage trustees at the monthly "Cookies and More with the Board" to demonstrate online registration.

EXTERNAL
- Send a news release to the local paper.
- Create a graphic with a link for the website on the library's home page.
- Revise the web address on all print materials to be consistent with the "Did you know?" message.
- Create and post instructions for online registration on the calendar page of the website.
- Create a screensaver image for all in-house e-net stations (approximately fifty computers) touting the "Did you know?" message.
- Give specially designed notepads with the message to those who participate in demonstrations.
- Post the message on the library's outdoor electronic sign.
- Make online program registration available from every computer in the library.
- Make announcements and conduct hands-on demonstrations at library programs such as movies and computer training.
- Install an additional computer near registration and circulation to facilitate demonstrations.
- Make signing up for a program online part of the adult summer reading program scavenger hunt.
- Encourage staff to promote the program as part of their activities in the community, such as hosting their own book groups, attending Kiwanis meetings, visiting the coffee shop, and banking.
- Staff a booth and talk up online registration at community events, including Earth Day and Welcome Neighbor, a village-sponsored program targeted to new residents.

Tools

- A "Did you know?" graphic for use on all promotional materials
- Signage (bright blue starbursts) on monitors throughout the building
- Scripts for staff on how to demonstrate online registration
- Bookmarks with a summary of the steps for online registration
- Sticky-note packs with the "Did you know?" message
- Brightly colored buttons for staff
- Giant cookies imprinted with the "Did you know?" graphic
- A dummy program for staff and the public to practice online registration

Budget

$100 for prizes ($50) and cookies ($50). The buttons, bookmarks, notepads, sticky notes, and signage were produced in-house.

Impact

We had very positive results. Patron registration for the month of June was 38 percent versus our 2006 baseline of 13 to 18 percent (depending on the month and the program). In April patron registration was at 29 percent. By June we had achieved a nine-point increase over April, representing an index of 131, surpassing our goal of a 25 percent increase in online registrations. We continue to see increases in online registration.

According to our postcampaign staff survey, 80 percent of the staff members are more comfortable talking about online registration with patrons. We significantly reduced the number of staff referring patrons to the registration desk, from 70 percent to only 19 percent, which means that fewer patrons are being bounced to another person when they want to register for a library program.

As part of this project, a computer was installed near registration to demonstrate how easy it is for patrons to register online for the library's programs. The staff at the registration desk and patrons found this computer so useful that it is now a permanent fixture in the lobby. This computer has greatly enhanced patron-staff interaction, providing an introduction and orientation to the library's services and offerings.

Last but not least, seventy-six participants—about 25 percent of our summer reading program participants—registered for a program online as part of the scavenger hunt!

Lessons Learned

Word-of-mouth marketing was a very effective tool for communicating this message. The price was right, and we proved that talking with users worked better than distributing fliers (our usual method). For patrons, the ability to discuss online registration provided a deeper understanding of the service than any written word ever could because it gave them the opportunity for two-way communication. For staff, it provided immediate positive feedback from patrons. In this viral, Web 2.0 world, it is important to remember that one-to-one communication plays a vital role in marketing any product or service, and word of mouth can be an effective tool. For libraries, staff members are their most influential ambassadors, and leveraging this role as a marketing tactic can be very effective.

One of the biggest surprises was what this promotion revealed about our patrons' behavior and their view of library programs. We learned that patrons enjoy library programs not just for their content but for the social aspect as well. We discovered this when we began using the patron version of E*vents (our online-registration software). As we demonstrated the program, patrons indicated their desire to sign up not only themselves but also three or four of their friends. The staff version of this software offers a field to indicate the number of attendees. This functionality was not available on the patron version of the software. Although the sign-up process was relatively simple for an individual, those attending in a group preferred to have staff sign them up.

Overall registrations initiated by patrons were at 38 percent for June; however, registrations ranged significantly by type of program. Programs targeted to young families and teens showed the highest usage of the patron-registration program. But programs with traditionally low online sign-ups also showed significant increases. For our daytime movie showings, which attract mainly senior citizens, online sign-ups doubled to 20 percent in June and July, from an average of 9 and 11 percent (April and May, respectively).

We were not entirely successful at reaching patrons outside the confines of the building. Staff members who wore the "Did you know?" buttons outside the building were, on occasion, questioned about the phrase, which provided an opportunity to discuss online registration. But staff members were generally not successful in initiating the discussion outside the building without this type of prompting. Reasons ranged from a lack of knowledge of upcoming programs to the fact that only 40 percent of staff are residents of the community and did not feel that the message was relevant to the people they encountered in their daily lives. Furthermore, despite training, not all of the staff felt comfortable initiating conversations with patrons, especially on subject matter outside their comfort zone or area of expertise.

We continue to encourage staff to look for opportunities to mention online registration and other aspects of the library in their conversations with friends, neighbors, and patrons.

—*Carolynn Muci, Marketing/Public Relations Director (cmuci@mppl.org)*

OAKTON COMMUNITY COLLEGE

This college library found faculty receptive to their message.

"You need to get other faculty members to talk about your programs and be willing to help others out by talking about their programs as well. Partnerships are very important."

Introduction

Oakton Community College (OCC) serves a community of almost 10,000 students at two campuses. Our main campus is in Des Plaines, and we have another campus in Skokie. Overall, there are more than 500 adjunct faculty members and about 150 full-time faculty.

We wanted to market our library and its resources to adjunct and part-time faculty in the hope that they would, in turn, encourage their students to use the library. We wanted to show them the benefits of library resources and how these resources might help students complete assignments in an efficient and effective way. If we successfully reached thirty faculty members, they might reach thirty students each via word of mouth, and so on. If adjunct faculty knew about our services, they might also put library assignments into their syllabi.

We focused on adjunct faculty because they are not on campus as much and are not as aware of what campus services are available. Also, adjunct faculty is the fastest-growing portion of the faculty, and we have new adjuncts all the time. The library needed an outreach program to address this reality so as to stay relevant to future instructors. When planning our strategies, the first thing we realized was that our target audience members were not likely to attend if they weren't compensated for their time, so we addressed that issue first. The Council of Deans readily approved our proposal.

Goal

Give adjunct faculty an overview of library services so that they would encourage their students to use the library.

Objectives

- Attract thirty faculty members to attend library-orientation workshops.
- Build awareness of library services among those who don't attend as well as those who do.
- Have faculty members give students extra credit as an incentive to attend library-training sessions.

Key Audiences

- College faculty, especially part-time and adjunct faculty
- Library faculty
- Deans and department chairs

Message

The library has resources to help your students succeed in their course work and prepare them for transfer to other schools or professional development.

Strategies

- Approach the Council of Deans about compensation for those attending workshops.
- Schedule five orientation workshops at various times, three at our Des Plaines campus and two at the Skokie campus.
- Send an invitation flier to all faculty members, both full- and part-time.
- Ask deans and department chairs to encourage attendance.
- Coordinate with Oakton's Center for Professional Development to promote the event, handle registration, and process evaluations.
- Ask the president of Oakton's Adjunct Faculty Association to encourage faculty to attend.
- Post an announcement on the library's web page.
- Involve all library faculty members in promoting workshops via word of mouth.
- Engage both full-time and adjunct library faculty to team-teach each workshop.

Tools

- Invitation flier
- An information packet of useful materials for each attendee
- Website announcement
- E-mail correspondence

Budget

Each workshop attendee was compensated about $30 for the 1.5-hour workshop, for an approximate budget of $1,200. All planning and staff implementation were done as part of our regular workload.

Impact

Forty faculty members attended our orientation workshops. All attendees received evaluation forms asking for their opinions of the workshop. There were many enthusiastic comments. Some of these faculty members have scheduled classes, and one instructor gave extra credit to students who came to the library. Some requested more advanced or specialized workshops in the future.

Another success was the variety of departments represented. We expected a good number of English, social science, and nursing faculty, but we also had attendees from departments that don't usually use the library, such as computer technologies.

After the workshops were over, we compiled an e-mail list, "Friends of the Oakton Library," which included all attendees, deans, and library faculty.

The OCC newspaper, the *Occurrence,* ran a piece in April 2007 about the library and the event, "Caught Talking about the Library," by Uri Toch.

We started using word-of-mouth strategies in other library marketing. For example, we had an orientation for student ambassadors to encourage them to talk up the library to their fellow students.

Lessons Learned

Adjunct faculty will come and learn about library resources when given an incentive. They are happy to look for ways to help their students use the library, as library usage has a positive impact on student learning.

Word of mouth is a cost-effective and labor-effective way of getting the word out. It is a very pliable strategy. For example, Uri Toch used word of mouth to build library awareness at College of Lake County (where he also works) by including positive library testimonials from users in e-mails to promote library training programs.

You need to be patient and keep trying. You need to get other faculty members to talk about your programs and be willing to help others out by talking about their programs as well. Partnerships are very important.

Next Steps

We plan to send brief, periodic e-mails letting all faculty members know of library activities and library news (e.g., new databases, books, videos, etc.). We hope to continually add to the list.

We also plan to take advantage of Oakton activities already in place, such as the New Faculty Seminar. We've contacted the coordinators of this series and have been invited to talk about the library and its resources.

We're also thinking of offering "house calls" by the library faculty to college administrators to show them how they can use the library from their offices (e.g., searching for articles in their favorite professional journals).

The Continuing Education Committee is planning a College Success seminar series, and we have contacted the coordinators and asked that the library be included. The College Success seminar attracts both full-time and part-time faculty.

—*Jane Malik, Assistant Professor, Library Services (jmalik@oakton.edu), and
Uri Toch, Librarian, Reference and Instruction (utoch@oakton.edu)*

TOWN AND COUNTRY PUBLIC LIBRARY (ELBURN)

Watson, the beloved "Golden Information Retriever" and library detective, both talks about the library and gives people something to talk about.

"Many parents comment on how kid-friendly our library is. Watson is a big part of that."

Introduction

A character never before seen now lives at the Town and Country Public Library. Watson is a "Golden Information Retriever" and library detective. He was created as part of our library's word-of-mouth marketing grant project. Watson lives in Friendlyville, the play area in the library's Youth Services Department, and carries a laptop computer he has nicknamed "Sherlock." Located about forty miles west of Chicago in Kane County, the Town and Country Public Library is a district library serving the Village of Elburn and portions of three townships and two school districts. Total population is about 10,000.

Goal

Create a welcoming image for kids and their families, encourage library use, and make the library more visible in the community.

Objectives

- Increase the library's presence in the community through appearances at special events and visits to schools and homebound patrons.
- Increase the number of library cards issued to children.
- Increase attendance at youth programs.
- Generate visits to the library's website, where the mascot will be featured.

Key Audiences

- Staff
- Friends
- Children
- Parents

Message

See you at the library!

Strategies

INTERNAL
- Train staff in word-of-mouth marketing techniques.
- Create a character to represent the library. Pick a name and develop character traits. Contact costume-design firm.
- Request the Friends of the Library to provide funding to create the library's new mascot—Watson, the "Golden Information Retriever" and library detective.
- Create a color illustration of Watson.
- Recruit and train volunteers to appear as Watson.
- Develop a basic script for Watson to use for at events, during promotions, on the library website, and on stationery.
- Have a private introduction of the mascot for staff, board members, and Friends of the Library.
- Introduce Watson at the Elburn Days Parade.

EXTERNAL
- Provide opportunities for patrons to meet Watson at the library. Everyone will receive autographed photos of our new mascot. Issue library cards to new patrons.
- Hand out bookmarks for twelve days with Watson's silhouette image and clues to who Watson is. Clues include "I love to read, especially mysteries," "I like to put puzzles together. It is like searching for clues," and "For exercise I love to play Frisbee." At the end of the twelve-day period, a picture of Watson will be revealed.
- Provide buttons with Watson's likeness and signature line for staff to wear.
- Place stories and advertisements in local newspapers, the library's newsletter, and school and community newsletters (ads also ran in back-to-school supplements).

WATSON'S BIOGRAPHY

- Age: seven. That's forty-nine in people years. Birthday: August 8.

- Favorite pastimes: putting together puzzles and playing Frisbee. Watson likes to put together puzzles. It's like searching for clues. He likes to exercise by playing Frisbee.

- Favorite books: mysteries, including *The Hound of the Baskervilles,* by Arthur Conan Doyle.

- Favorite foods and beverages: gourmet burgers and French bottled water.

- Favorite greeting to readers: "See you at the library!"

- Favorite color: red! Why red? Because Watson has read a lot! :)

- Watson enjoys long rides in convertible cars because he loves the feeling of the wind in his ears.

- Watson loves a parade! Every summer he rides in a red convertible in the Elburn Days Parade.

- Watson loves to receive his own e-mail.

- Watson loves hugs.

- Watson loves to visit children, moms and dads, and grandparents.

FIGURE 5.3 "See you at the library!" is the message that Watson, the beloved mascot for the Elburn, Illinois, Town and Country Public Library, delivers.

Reproduced with permission of the library.

- Place Watson's photographs, biography, and coloring pages on his own web page (Wide World of Watson) on the library's website.
- Create an e-mail address for Watson so children can send their reference questions.
- Schedule appearances for our mascot. These include Elburn Days (annual community weekend), the Elburn Chamber of Commerce Christmas Stroll, Dewey Dash (the library's annual 5-K run and one-mile walk), storytimes and craft workshops at the library, and school visits.

Tools

- T-shirts with Watson's likeness for staff, board members, Friends of the Library, and volunteers
- Giveaways for the public—bookmarks, photographs, buttons, T-shirts, pencils, stickers, and stuffed dolls
- Pictures of Watson's silhouette for display throughout the library
- Buttons for staff
- Pencil box for children signing up for their first library card. The cover of the box has a drawing of Watson along with his favorite saying: "See you at the library!"

Budget

We estimate that the cost for the creation of the concept, costume, carrying case, and miscellaneous equipment was approximately $3,000.

Impact

We have realized our four objectives. Many parents comment on how kid-friendly our library is. Watson is a big part of that. Nearly everyone in the community knows who Watson is. He has been a hit with kids and adults since he made his debut, riding in a red convertible in the Elburn Days parade in August 2007. When he made his second appearance, in August 2008, all of the children knew his name. A musician scheduled to appear at the library wrote a song in his honor. (You can hear it on the library's website, at www.elburn.lib .il.us/youth/watson.htm.) Another nice surprise was the very generous funding for the mascot provided by the Friends of the Library. We now have four volunteers willing to portray Watson.

Watson is prominently featured on the library's website and has a full calendar. He has been invited twice to the first day of school at Lily Lake Grade School, one of the three elementary schools served by our library. He dons a Halloween outfit and participates in Halloween parties with children attending the library's storytimes and kindergarten-readiness classes. Watson also welcomes Santa, Mrs. Claus, and more than 1,000 guests to the library for the annual Elburn Chamber of Commerce Christmas Stroll. For the past several years, Town and Country Public Library has kicked off National Library Week with the Dewey Dash, a 5-K run and one-mile walk that attracts runners and walkers from across the Midwest. Last year Watson donned red running shorts and red sneakers to be the lead runner in the race! Watson greets student groups that come through the library. And, of course, we celebrate his birthday (August 8) with cookies and ice cream.

Lessons Learned

The most challenging aspect of this project was to develop the mascot. The entire staff went through several weeks of brainstorming sessions before we finally settled on our mascot.

We would advise libraries that are considering a mascot to allow about a year for the project to come to fruition.

—Dwayne Nelson, Youth Services and
Reference Librarian (dnelson@elburn.lib.il.us)

WARRENVILLE PUBLIC LIBRARY

A tight focus paid off for this library's first buzz venture.

"It's always rewarding when a patron comes to us and the first words he or she speaks are, 'A friend told me . . .' That's when we know our word-of-mouth efforts are paying off."

Introduction

The Warrenville Public Library District serves about 14,000 residents in suburban Chicago. Frustrated with low usage statistics for costly online databases, librarians wanted to be sure patrons were aware of the rich resources available on the library's website. Rather than try to reach a broad audience and talk about "databases," staff decided to try a focused approach. They selected a target audience (students) and specific resources (online tutoring and encyclopedias) that would be valued by their audience. In addition to educating the chosen audience, the program was also designed to introduce frontline circulation staff to the same resources so they could promote the resources to patrons visiting the library.

Goal

The goal of the Warrenville Public Library District's word-of-mouth marketing (WOMM) project was to get the word out about online databases that are available for free to any library cardholder twenty-four hours a day, seven days a week. The library wanted to increase the use of these databases, which are costly yet underutilized.

Objectives

- Increase the use of our targeted databases by 10 percent.
- Collect at least twenty-five testimonials about the databases.

Key Audiences

- Library staff
- Fourth-grade students and teachers
- Parents

Message

Get Smart about Homework @ www.warrenville.com

Strategies

- Teach staff about our databases and basic WOMM techniques, including how to recognize opportunities both in the library *and* in the community.
- Visit fourth-grade classrooms to promote our databases.
- Create and distribute informational materials about the databases during school visits and demonstrations. These materials are also available at the library and are used for staff training purposes.
- Create an overview sheet informing parents of the free online resources available for their children. Include information on how to get a library card. Conduct a follow-up online survey with students to gather information about which online services they used, if they felt the services were helpful, and whether they would tell a friend about the library's website.
- Place articles in various media outlets, including newspapers and the local public-access cable channel.

Tools

- PowerPoint presentation
- Information packets for students, teachers, and parents
- "Get Smart" buttons for kids

Budget

The library spent approximately $150 for the first year of the program. This included folders for the information sheets, buttons for the students, and gift cards for the students who completed an online survey. Ongoing costs are minimal, less than $50 per year.

Impact

The most successful aspects of our project included the narrow focus of our word-of-mouth campaign, the connections we made with teachers and librarians at the schools we visited, and the groundwork we've laid for the future. The introduction to word-of-mouth marketing reinforced what many of our staff were already doing—only now they have a name for it.

Library staff had not conducted regular school visits for several years. This program allowed us to reconnect with school staff, especially the school librarian, and increase our visibility with teachers and students. Although the teachers knew about our "traditional" resources, the demonstration we conducted at the schools made the teachers aware of additional resources that they could recommend to their students.

Other outcomes:

Usage of the three databases we promoted spiked in the two weeks following our school presentations. Weekly use increased from three to ten users per week to an average of about thirty users per week. Usage quickly fell off as we approached the end of the school year.

Staff became familiar with the databases and can now point library users to appropriate online resources.

We've adapted the "Get Smart" phrase on promotional pieces for our other electronic resources—"Get Smart about Genealogy" promotes Ancestry.com;

"Get Smart about Literature" promotes NoveList; and so forth. It's an easy phrase to remember and ties in well with the topics covered by our electronic resources.

The timing for this project was not ideal as we were presenting homework-help tips in the spring, when school was winding down in May. We had a minimal response collecting testimonials through our online survey—this is best done on an informal basis in a one-on-one situation. However, we now have a great plan in place that can be easily implemented at the beginning of the school year from now on.

Lessons Learned

The library now visits fourth-grade classrooms every fall. In addition, we've placed print advertising in the high school newspaper and have purchased custom-printed notepads to promote several of our online services. Whenever we reintroduce a service or do something different to promote it, we see a spike in the usage statistics. Perhaps the biggest lesson we've learned is that the message has to be meaningful to the audience. Staff are always listening for "cues" from our patrons so that they can "buzz" about specific programs and services. It's always rewarding when a patron comes to us and the first words he or she speaks are, "A friend told me . . ." That's when we know our word-of-mouth efforts are paying off.

—Sandy Whitmer, Library Director (director@warrenville.com)

WAUKEGAN PUBLIC LIBRARY

This library successfully harnessed the power of word-of-mouth marketing to raise funds for an Early Learning Center.

"The most important part of the process was laying the groundwork. Once that was done and the initial contacts made, it took on a life of its own."

Introduction

Located in one of Illinois's oldest communities, the Waukegan Public Library serves a population of just over 90,000 residents. It has been involved in an award-winning adult literacy program for more than twenty-three years and family literacy for eighteen years. However, the city still has eight schools listed as "School Improvement Status" that have been identified by the No Child Left Behind Act. Within the school district, 43 percent of the children are identified as low income, and the high school has only a 67 percent graduation rate. More than 71 percent of the children are Hispanic, 18 percent are African American, and 7 percent are Caucasian. Thirty-two percent have limited English and are eligible for bilingual instruction.

The library chose to use word-of-mouth marketing (WOMM) primarily to raise awareness of and funds for the building of an Early Learning Center (ELC) devoted to preschool literacy. Through more than sixty-four community presentations reaching more than 1,200 people, events at local restaurants, community partnerships, churches, programs, paper and cell-phone recycling, and much more—and with a budget of only $5,000 over two years—the staff of the library successfully educated the community about the need for early literacy and the opening of the ELC while raising more than $200,000.

Goal

Create a buzz and win support through funding for our new Early Learning Center prior to breaking ground.

Objectives

- Win support from city leaders.
- Begin a fund-raising campaign.
- Recruit community partners to ensure success.
- Educate staff, board, volunteers, and Friends so they can spread the word.
- Build staff's confidence and skills in doing word-of-mouth marketing.

Key Audiences

- Staff
- Library and foundation board members, volunteers, and Friends
- Community leaders
- Community partners in education

Message

Did you hear what we are doing now? We want to build Sesame Street you can visit.

Strategies

- Kick off campaign in April.
- Use children's building blocks to visually market the campaign.
- Provide word-of-mouth training for staff, volunteers, Friends, and library and foundation board.
- Use staff newsletter to keep the buzz going.
- Provide "What are we doing next?" buttons for staff to wear.
- Give out cards at the circulation desk with a link to a web page explaining plans for the Early Learning Center.
- Create a special website with continuous updates.
- Prepare a PowerPoint presentation for showing to library and community groups.
- Place articles in community newspapers and newsletters.
- Provide fliers to schools for children to take home.
- Create and send holiday cards.

Tools

- PowerPoint presentation
- Posters
- Exhibits
- Handouts and fliers

Budget

A total of $4,900 was spent on printing, posters, donor stewardship, and web updates over two years. An additional $2,000 was spent in fall 2008 on a contract writer, bringing the total budget to around $7,000, not including staff time.

Impact

- We made sixty-four community presentations, reaching more than 1,200 people.
- New partnerships were formed with local businesses, banks, and individuals.
- We raised $200,000 in 1.5 years. The public awareness and fund-raising campaign paid off with two-thirds of the money raised for the room.
- Our campaign also had an impact on attendance once the room was open. Prior to the ELC opening, there were four storytimes with 46 adults and 80 children attending. In November, there were 55 story-times with 208 adults and 252 children.
- Staff benefited from both the training and the execution of WOMM. They felt more involved and prepared to promote the ELC. Many took it upon themselves to raise funds on their own by promoting the project to their friends and family. Allowing our staff to donate sick or vacation time to the fund-raising project helped them to feel more involved.
- WOMM helped keep our costs low.

Lessons Learned

The most important part of the process was laying the groundwork. Once that was done and the initial contacts made, it took on a life of its own. We were surprised how easy it is once your presentation is prepared. Simply by asking each group or individual we spoke to for another contact kept the momentum going.

Word-of-mouth marketing does work, but it is very time intensive for staff. However, the benefits of connecting to the community on a personal level will have an enormous payoff in partnerships, donations, and, hopefully, more people using the library.

It is also important to keep a database of contacts for future reference.

Consider using secret shoppers to find out if your staff is "on message."

—*Elizabeth Stearns, Assistant Director, Community Services*
(estearns@waukeganpl.info)

WINNETKA-NORTHFIELD PUBLIC LIBRARY DISTRICT

Both online use and staff morale got a boost when this library focused on engaging staff.

"Our staff were excited by the incentive contests and by the database training. Once they felt comfortable using the resources, they were able to pass the key message on with confidence."

Introduction

The Winnetka-Northfield Public Library District encompasses two highly educated, affluent communities on the North Shore of Chicago. The community is known for its outstanding schools, including the nationally recognized New Trier High School. The library serves a population of 17,808, with median family incomes over $100,000. Our library has great customer service and excellent resources, but we needed to generate greater awareness of its online resources. Although 85 percent of the district has library cards, our cardholders don't use their online resources as well as they could. This project was designed to increase both staff and patron awareness of the library's online services by revamping the way our message is delivered to busy residents.

Goals

- Patrons of the Winnetka-Northfield Public Library District will value and use their library 24/7.
- Our staff will have exceptional customer service skills.
- The staff and board will deliver a clear, concise message with accuracy and confidence.

Objectives

- Increase staff knowledge and comfort level by providing training about the library's databases, word-of-mouth marketing, and customer service techniques.
- Increase the number of unique cardholder hits to the online resources by 10 percent.
- Increase the number of consultations about various online services.

Key Audiences

- Staff
- Trustees
- Influential members of the community
- Winnetka Chamber of Commerce
- Northfield Chamber of Commerce
- Winnetka Alliance for Early Childhood
- Rotary of Winnetka-Northfield
- Parents
- Elementary- and middle-school children.

Message

We're Up When You Are! 24 Hours a Day.

Strategies

INTERNAL
- Provide training for staff on word-of-mouth marketing and the importance of team involvement, also online resources, customer service, and one of our newest databases, Standard and Poor's.
- Encourage staff to explore these resources individually and to familiarize themselves with one or two databases on their own.
- Hold a contest to promote staff involvement in developing and delivering our message.
- Survey staff pre- and post-training to gauge comfort level with word-of-mouth marketing and the library's databases.
- Provide cheat sheets with talking points to help staff initiate conversations. These were designed specifically for nonreference staff members who don't deal with reference interviews or databases on a regular basis.

EXTERNAL

- Develop and distribute a handy "24-Hour Resources" bookmark-checklist that lists our online services.
- Encourage staff to talk up and demonstrate online databases to library users at every opportunity. Give notepad cubes to those who participate. Staff members who give away the most notepads will win prizes.
- Expand database training for public to include our newest database, Standard and Poor's. This database was added as a direct result of a conversation at the Northfield Branch during the incentive contest.
- Participate in special events (e.g., first-grade reading parties, the Chamber of Commerce Annual Sidewalk Sale). Provide goodie bags with promotional materials, including a coupon for a consultation with a librarian.

Tools

- A $50 gift card for the best slogan or message submitted by staff
- Notepad cubes with our message on them
- Laminated cheat sheets with talking points
- The "24-Hour Resources" bookmark-checklist (Worth its weight in gold, this bookmark lists all of the library's 24-hour online resources with boxes for staff to check off suggested databases when conversing with patrons.)
- Coupons for an hour of personal consultation time with a librarian

Budget

$2,450 was spent on staff incentives, promo items, and staff training.

Impact

The most successful aspect of this project was the staff involvement. Thirty-four staff members and three board members were trained during seven sessions on word-of-mouth marketing, customer service, and online resources. Surveys showed staff's comfort levels increased significantly over the course of the grant period. Our staff were excited by the incentive contests and by the database training. Once they felt comfortable using the resources, they were able to pass the key message on with confidence. We continue to hold refresher training sessions.

The number of hits by unique cardholders was more than double what we had projected. It increased by 23 percent between March and April after staff training took place. Database usage increased 14.6 percent from October 2007 to October 2008.

During the incentive contest, which lasted a week, staff distributed 160 promotional notepad cubes to the public. Two staff members were awarded $50 gift cards from Barnes and Noble for their efforts. One distributed fifty-six cubes. She said she liked having a reason to initiate talking with customers. Hundreds of the "24-Hour Resources" bookmarks were given out.

The least successful aspect was the coupon promotion. Not a single coupon for a consultation was returned. We suspect this is because people did not feel a need for a coupon and would turn to us anyway.

This marketing project marked the start of revamping the way the Winnetka-Northfield Public Library District delivers the message about 24/7 services to our busy residents. By continually increasing both staff and patron awareness,

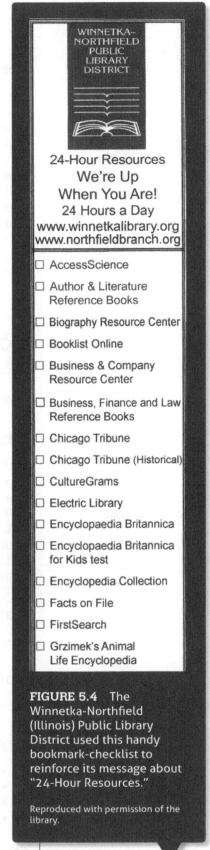

FIGURE 5.4 The Winnetka-Northfield (Illinois) Public Library District used this handy bookmark-checklist to reinforce its message about "24-Hour Resources."

Reproduced with permission of the library.

we want to inform people that our exceptional customer service extends into their homes via our website. And then we want them to tell their friends . . .

Lessons Learned

One challenge was to overcome staff's assumption that good customer service is enough. It was important to stress that marketing has become an integral part of everyday business at the library. The phrase "promotes library services and materials" has been added to all staff evaluation forms.

It was surprising and rewarding to see the way people responded to being part of the team. It was a positive experience for all the staff to see how their colleagues, even those who are shy, excelled at being customer service extroverts. People learned from each other. This was the perfect project to foster team building from within the ranks.

The "24-Hour Resources" bookmark-checklist has become one of our most useful promotional pieces. It can be adapted for a variety of situations and uses by any department. It is simple and easy to replicate for any library.

—*Juli Janovicz, Head of Adult Services (julij@wpld.alibrary.com)*

ZION-BENTON PUBLIC LIBRARY

When this library buzzed about self-check, people listened.

"What's the Buzz? It works. And it's cheap to do."

Introduction

Our library serves 43,000 people in the far north suburbs outside Chicago. It serves a diverse population, with 70 percent Caucasian, 18 percent African American, and 12 percent Hispanic patrons.

This project, dubbed "Plan Bee," used our community's symbol—a bee—to build a buzz. Masterminded by the library's Circ and Technical Services departments, the project focused on educating and encouraging library visitors to use self-checkout. It also served as a model for putting word-of-mouth marketing to work in other library departments.

Goal

Educate library users about the library's self-checkout machine.

Objective

Increase use of self-checkout.

Key Audiences

- All staff, particularly at the circulation desk
- Board of directors
- Friends of the Library
- Library users

Message

What's the buzz? Ask us!

Strategies

INTERNAL
- Make a presentation about self-check at the board's monthly meeting.
- Recruit board members to assist in teaching patrons to use the self-checkout machine.
- Encourage Friends to talk up self-checkout.
- Provide training in word-of-mouth marketing for all staff.

EXTERNAL
- Promote self-checkout in the library newsletter.
- Place a story in the local newspaper.
- Hold a free raffle for all library users with easy tips for using self-check on the back of entry slips. We hid these generously throughout the library.
- Create a bee logo to help build the buzz. All buttons, coupons, raffle tickets, and signage were yellow and black and featured the bee logo.
- Create signage and handouts with the bee logo and message.
- Include the message on the receipt printer.
- Create a display near the reference desk with a giant bee.
- Provide "What's the Buzz?" buttons for staff to wear to encourage inquiries.

Tools

- Free video coupons for staff who participated in word-of-mouth marketing training
- Buttons for staff
- Signage and handouts with the bee logo and message
- The "Big Bee" (a large papier-mâché bee displayed on the circ desk)
- Raffle tickets with talking points on the back
- A banner with the "bee logo" above the self-checkout machine

Budget

We used materials we already had in our graphics room.

Impact

What's the Buzz? It works. And it's cheap to do. What was most successful? An actual demonstration of the power of an organized, focused, consistent, measurable word-of-mouth marketing effort. Use of self-checkout increased dramatically. We experienced a 44 percent increase in patron use and a 44 percent increase in the number of items checked out compared to the comparable time frame from the year before. Total item circulation for self-checkout was 14 percent of total item circulation compared to 8 percent prior to Plan Bee. We enjoyed seeing many patrons using the self-checkout for the first time. Some were so small they could barely see over the top of the cart, and one person was in his nineties.

Other departments have done "buzzes." For example, Adult Services promoted the generic paperbacks, and Youth Services did an "I spy" wall (kind of like "Where's Waldo?") to promote the summer reading club. Staff still say, "We should do a buzz about that" whenever we feel we need to educate the public.

Lessons Learned

We had expected to schedule staff, board members, and volunteers to assist patrons in the use of the machine. This did not materialize. Perhaps the timing of the event was poor, because there were many other programs happening at the same time. In the end, patron assistance was on an informal basis. We did see this happening often, and it seems to have been quite effective. Also, our patrons can only use self-checkout for books. We found that if patrons were able to use self-checkout for more types of items, it would be used more often.

—*Rosemary Kauth, Circulation and Technical Services Coordinator (rkauth@zblibrary.org) and Debbie Potocek, Technical Services Associate (dpotocek@zblibrary.org)*

CHAPTER 6

Power Pack

The following tools are provided to help you and your staff harness the power of word-of-mouth marketing.

MARKETING TERMS AND DEFINITIONS

Advertising: The placement and purchase of time or space for announcements and messages in the media.

Advocacy: Persuasive communication designed to plead or make the case for a cause or point of view. Libraries and other nonprofit organizations use advocacy to win support for funding and other issues that affect their users.

Brand: Brand is another word for identity as conveyed in print and other communications. A logo and slogan/tagline help to convey identity.

Community relations: How a library interacts in the locality in which it operates.

Direct marketing: Promotion designed to go directly to a target audience—generally direct mail.

E-marketing: Reaching out to particular markets of users and potential users using the Internet as a communications and distribution channel.

Lobbying: A form of advocacy intended to influence the outcome of particular legislation. It is subject to IRS guidelines. A lobbyist is a professional communicator hired to persuade lawmakers and shape public opinion.

Market: Potential users or customers.

Marketing mix: A mix of controllable variables that may be used to reach goals and objectives. Core variables include price, product, place, and promotion.

Point of purchase: Promotional materials placed at the contact "sales" point to attract user interest or call attention to a special offer.

Positioning: How you want users and potential users to perceive your product or service—what separates it from the competition.

Public relations: All the ways that your library relates to and communicates with the public, including community and campus outreach, customer service, and the media.

Word-of-mouth marketing isn't about you and your brand. It's about them—the people who will start the conversation for you.

—Mark Hughes,
Buzzmarketing:
Get People to Talk
about Your Stuff

Publicity: Communications intended to promote your products or services that do not involve paid advertising (e.g., news releases, public service announcements, fliers, posters).

Strategic marketing plan: The entire marketing process, including researching, designing, developing and distributing products and services, communicating the value, and evaluating the success of these efforts.

Target audience/market: A segment of the population selected as the focus of a marketing effort in order to accomplish the stated objectives.

Tchotchke: Based on a Yiddish word. Commonly used in the PR biz to refer to small giveaway items like key rings, pencils, and magnets.

Word-of-mouth marketing (WOMM): The organized, conscious, consistent approach to getting others to deliver your message for you.

Adapted from the "Section on Management and Marketing: Glossary of Marketing Definitions," IFLANET, http://archive.ifla.org/VII/s34/pubs/glossary.htm, developed by using Peter Bennett's Dictionary of Marketing Terms, 2nd ed. (New York: McGraw-Hill, 1995).

A WORD-OF-MOUTH MARKETING CHECKLIST

☐ Do you have a clear, consistent, and compelling message—one that can be said at the checkout desk or in a grocery-store checkout line?

☐ Do the people at the checkout desk know and deliver the message?

☐ Do you collect and use testimonials and success stories?

☐ Do you use outside experts to deliver your message?

☐ Do staff collect and feed back what they hear—both good and bad?

☐ Do you have a prepared and enthusiastic sales force?

☐ Does your library give superlative customer service?

☐ Is conscious word of mouth part of your promotion strategies?

Adapted from *The Secrets of Word-of-Mouth Marketing: How to Trigger Exponential Sales through Runaway Word of Mouth*, by George Silverman (New York: AMACOM, 2001).

SAMPLE COMMUNICATION PLAN

From Winnetka-Northfield (Illinois) Public Library District

1. Introduction

Patrons continue to express surprise about the availability of 24/7 online resources and the website. We need to change the way our message is delivered to our busy patrons!

Strengths

> Knowledgeable staff
> Great customer service
> Excellent array of databases and online resources
> Available 24/7
> Strong PR focus

Strong vendor commitment and support
Good web support
Safe, accurate, reliable information
Passage of successful referendum

Weaknesses

PR isn't connecting
Busy patrons with time constraints
Information overload
Just Google it!
Layout of newsletter, website
Physical size of buildings
Large number of cardholders who don't use our online resources
Lack of training—staff
Lack of training—public

Opportunities

Large number of registered borrowers
Large number of computer users
Community support (e.g., successful referendum)
Community partnerships (e.g., local schools, Chambers of
    Commerce, etc.)
Help staff grow and become integral part of PR endeavor

Threats

Information overload
Google
Affluence
Library seen as unnecessary
Wealthy buy access to online
Wealthy buy access to books
One-time bad customer service in person
One-time bad online experience
Staff not buying in

2. Goals

- Develop a clear, concise message that can be used by staff anywhere,
  anytime.
- Make patrons more aware of online resources.
- Make staff buy into big picture and deliver message with accuracy
  and confidence.

3. Objectives

- Increase staff knowledge and comfort level with online resources by
  holding training sessions.
- Increase the number of unique cardholder hits to the online
  resources.
- Measure staff participation by counting the number of promotional
  items distributed to patrons during a contest.
- Count the number of coupons redeemed from the May–June
  promotion.

4. Positioning Statement

We're the Nordstrom's of the North Shore. "Let your librarian be your personal shopper."

5. Key Message

We're Up When You Are! 24 Hours a Day. www.winnetkalibrary.org

6. Key Audiences

Staff, board, patrons, parents, students (middle and elementary)

7. Strategies/Action Plan

January 2007

> Presentations/contest
> Key message contest for staff
> Presentation/training at staff meeting outlining word-of-mouth and
>   buzz marketing; staff incentive $50

April 2007

> Presentations/training
> Word-of-mouth presentations outlining talking points and demonstra-
>   tions/training on online resources for staff and board $0

May 2007

> Presentations/training
> Customer service training for staff $1,800
> Staff contest for distributing promotional items to patrons
> Promotional items $400
> Staff incentives for contest $200

May–June 2007

> Coupon promotions via newsletter (patrons) and first-grade reading
>   party materials (parents); allow coupons to be redeemed for one-on-
>   one consulting time (personal shopping) with librarian
> Budget in place

July 2007

> Compile statistics for grant report

July 2007

> Redesign website
> Integrate key message into design
> Develop and distribute materials to media
> $10,000 + (Budget 07–08)

Fall 2007

> Fund-raising letter distributed to all households in the two villages;
>   integrate key message "We're Up When You Are! 24 Hours a Day"
> Continue to repeat key message

8. Evaluation Measures

- Statistics gathered from the website re: the number of unique card-holders
- Number of coupons redeemed for personalized services
- Number of promotional items handed out
- Patron feedback
- Staff feedback

SAMPLE STAFF SURVEY

Be sure to address internal communication as part of your communication plan. As part of your project evaluation, you might begin with a very brief survey like this one and do it again post-training.

1. Do you make a point of telling library users about other services that might be of interest to them (e.g., databases, e-books, etc.)?

    No   Sometimes   Often

2. Do you make a point of telling your friends/neighbors/others in the community about what the library offers?

    No   Sometimes   Often

3. Do you encourage other people, especially satisfied customers, to tell others about library services?

    No   Sometimes   Often

4. Do you collect and report compliments that you hear from library visitors?

    No   Sometimes   Often

5. How confident do you feel delivering the library's message?

    Not at all   Some   Enough   Very

6. Do you feel you have enough information?

    Yes   No   Sometimes

7. What would help you feel more confident in talking about the library?

    More training   Message sheet   Other?

8. Please share any suggestions for how we can support you in getting the word out about the library.

Thank you!

SAMPLE Q&A

The Crystal Lake (Illinois) Public Library prepared this script to help staff deal with questions about its remodeling project (see chapter 5).

Bad Example

Patron: What's up with this Project Shoehorn?

Staff: Project Shoehorn is a big construction project we have coming up. We're getting new desks and totally revamping our employee workspaces. They are bringing in work crews to remodel the library so that we won't have any more issues about too little space. This should take care of our space issues for a L-O-N-G time.

Patron: I knew we didn't need a bigger library.

Good Example

Patron: What's up with this Project Shoehorn?

Staff: Project Shoehorn is a temporary solution to our space needs. We're reorganizing our library to give us up to five more years in the current building without a major expansion.

Patron: What will happen?

Staff: We'll be bringing our adult collections together on one level, and youth services will move to the lower level. We'll be working on maximizing our shelving space and providing a wireless network for the public. Here's a schedule of our planned library closings and the times when we'll have reduced library services.

SAMPLE AGENDA FOR INTRODUCTORY STAFF WORKSHOP

Use this sample agenda to create your own program. (Sample scenarios are found below, under "Sample Scripts.")

Building a Buzz

Objectives
- Teach staff basic WOMM techniques and their role in it.
- Engage staff in buzzing about your library.

I.   Welcome/Introduction (30 min.)

- What is marketing?
- Why you need a team
- Turning customers into champions

II. Introduction to Word-of-Mouth Marketing (30 min.)

- What it is
- Why it's powerful

- How to do it
- Must-haves
- Motivating staff

III. What's Our Message? (30 min.)

- Brainstorm ideas, strategies, and tools for delivering it

IV. Delivering the Message (30 min.)

- Delivery techniques
- Dealing with the negative
- Scenarios: library sales force in action

V. Wrap Up (10 min.)

- Questions/concerns
- Evaluation
- Next steps

REALLY GOOD RESOURCES

ALA Store, www.alastore.ala.org.
Order ALA's celebrity READ posters or a CD with reproducible graphics to make your own. There are also hats, buttons, bookmarks, T-shirts, and a wealth of other promotional items to help you deliver your message with pizzazz.

***Buzz Marketing: Get People to Talk about Your Stuff,* by Mark Hughes (New York, Penguin, 2005).**
Read this overview. Enjoy lots of great examples and think about them, because this is the world we live in.

Buzz Grant Project, www.nsls.info/buzzmarketing/.
Learn more about the North Suburban Library System and DuPage Library System project.

CLASS (Customers Leaving Appreciative, Satisfied, and Sold)
One of the best library customer service programs we've seen—and they're willing to share. A kit, which includes a CD and thirty-six-page manuals for both the trainer and participants, can be ordered ($299) from CLASS, Columbus Metropolitan Library, 96 S. Grant Avenue, Columbus, OH 43215. Telephone: 614-849-1089.

***Controlling the Confrontation: Arch Lustberg on Effective Communication Techniques* (Baltimore: Library Video Network, 1989). Video.**
One of our all-time favorites. The techniques Lustberg shares are tailored to libraries.

***How to Say It: Marketing with New Media; A Guide to Promoting Your Small Business Using Websites, E-zines, Blogs, and Podcasts,* by Lena Claxton and Alison Wood (New York: Prentice Hall, 2008).**
A readable and informative introduction to various types of online media and how to use them effectively.

Libraries, Mission and Marketing: Writing Mission Statements That Work, by Linda K. Wallace (Chicago: American Library Association, 2004).
The premise of this book is that your library's mission statement should be its key message. You should be able to say what you do—and do as you say.

Mission-Based Marketing, How Your Not-for-Profit Can Succeed in a More Competitive World, by Peter C. Brinckerhoff (New York: Wiley, 1997).
Clear, step-by-step guide to identifying and understanding your markets, considering the competition, needs vs. wants, and lots more. Practical and interesting.

The Secrets of Word-of-Mouth Marketing: How to Trigger Exponential Sales through Runaway Word of Mouth, by George Silverman (New York: AMACOM, 2001).
Silverman says traditional advertising doesn't have the impact it once did, and makes a great case for an organized, strategic approach to word of mouth. This is good news for libraries since we couldn't afford advertising anyway.

Word-of-Mouth Marketing, by Jerry R. Wilson (New York: Wiley, 1991).
This excellent text includes the pyramid model about turning customers into champions—powerful advice for libraries.

Word-of-Mouth Marketing: How Smart Companies Get People Talking, by Andy Sernovitz (New York: Kaplan, 2006).
More insights into WOMM from the CEO of the Word of Mouth Marketing Association.

Word of Mouth Marketing Association, http://womma.org.
Word of mouth has its own, relatively new association with many excellent resources online. Check it out.

SAMPLE SCRIPTS

Use these scripts "as is" or invent your own to spark conversation with your staff about WOMM. And yes, they're exaggerated in order to make the point. Questions to ask: What did you see happening in this scenario? What techniques were used? Was the spokesperson prepared? Enthusiastic? Proactive? Did you hear a message? What else might the Library Super Salesperson (LSS) have done/said?

Scenario I: Guys/Gals in the Locker Room

There's just about no place you can't buzz—with or without clothes. Here the Library Super Salesperson (LSS)—could be a Friend or trustee—is in the locker room at the gym. A gal/guy opens the locker next to him/her. Informal, conversational tone throughout.

LSS *(smiling):* Sorry if I'm in your way.

Guy/Gal: No problem.

LSS: I'm [name]. I don't remember seeing you around. Are you new here?

Guy/Gal: Actually, I am. My name's [name]. I just moved here from Columbus.

LSS: Welcome! I think you'll like it here. It's a great community. What brought you this way?

Guy/Gal: I'm a real-estate agent. I'm going into business with my brother.

LSS: Have you been to the library by any chance? I work there.

Guy/Gal: Actually, I haven't.

LSS: You should check it out. It's a real selling point for our community. And we're open 24/7 online.

Guy/Gal: That sounds excellent.

LSS *(pulls out business card):* Here, take my card. I'd be glad to give you a tour.

Guy/Gal *(extending hand):* Thanks. Maybe I'll do that. Good meeting you!!

Scenario II: Testimonial

The Library Super Salesperson closes the transaction by asking the very satisfied customer for a testimonial.

LSS: There you go! This book and these three websites should have everything you need.

User: Oh my goodness, you are amazing!!! I knew there was a lot of stuff out there about doing your family tree . . . But when I went online, I was overwhelmed. At least now I know where to start. Thank you so much!!!

LSS (*smiling, open face*): I'm glad I could help. But now I have a question for you. I'd like to write down what you just said and have you sign this permission form. We love to have stories like yours to share.

User (*somewhat reluctant*): Well . . .

LSS: I think what you said was, "Oh my goodness, you are amazing!!! I knew there was a lot of stuff out there about doing your family tree . . . But when I went online, I was overwhelmed. At least now I know where to start. Thank you so much!!!" Would it be OK if we quote you? It's for a good cause.

User: Oh, I guess I can do that. You really are amazing!!!

Scenario III: Reluctant Student

A not-very-enthusiastic student approaches a librarian. The LSS keeps a casual, friendly tone throughout and is prepared to take advantage of this opportunity to buzz about databases.

Student: I need everything you've got about women who served in the Civil War.

LSS *(smiling, open face):* Sounds like you're writing a paper.

Student *(unenthusiastically):* Afraid so.

LSS: Do you use the library much?

Student: Not unless I have to. I get pretty much everything I need on the Internet.

LSS: Yeah, the Internet is great! But sometimes books are better, especially when it comes to things like history. I'd be glad to help you find something . . . By the way, do you know about our databases?

Student: I've heard about 'em . . . Didn't know the library had any.

LSS: The databases are very cool. They're on our website, and you can find a lot of stuff you won't find on the Internet. Let me show you. Then you can show your friends.

Student: Thanks a lot!

Scenario IV: Welcome, Neighbor!

Yet another way to build a buzz. The LSS—could be a Friend or trustee—is knocking at a new neighbor's door with a welcome plate of cookies and some literature about the library. The neighbor is still unpacking and a bit distracted. There are sounds of a baby crying and a dog barking in the background. This could also be adapted for welcoming a new principal or faculty member.

Neighbor *(arms crossed, harried expression):* Hello? (Will you guys please be quiet?!! There's someone at the door.)

LSS *(smiling, open face):* Hi!! I'm [name], your neighbor from across the street. Welcome to our neighborhood!! I brought you some cookies.

Neighbor *(smiling, uncrosses arms):* That's very nice of you. Thanks!! Would you like to come in?

LSS *(enthusiastically):* That's OK. You've got your hands full. I thought you could probably use a treat—and I thought you should know about our wonderful library. I'm on the board.

Neighbor *(not very interested):* Really! Our old library wasn't that great.

LSS: Well, this one is fabulous!! We've got books, CDs, DVDs, computers, and an incredible website. We've also got some great programs for kids.

Neighbor: That does sound good. Where is it?

LSS *(pointing):* It's over there a couple miles. I brought you a map and one of our library guides. I'd be glad to show you around.

Neighbor: That's very kind of you. Thanks so much.

Scenario V: Unhappy Mom—Wrong Way

There are two versions of this script. In this version, a not-so-super library staff member is shelving books when an irate mother accosts him or her. The tone is confrontational. Body and face language are closed on both sides. The mother arrives and leaves upset. Discuss what went wrong. Then perform the "Right Way."

Mother *(angry tone):* I just have to tell someone. I am *so* upset!!! My son had a paper due today, but when we came to the library yesterday, it was closed. I couldn't believe it. How could the library not be open on Sunday???? The day when all kids are doing their homework.

LSS *(folds arms across chest):* Sorry about that, but we've been closed Fridays and Sundays ever since the voters turned down our tax increase. A lot of people aren't happy.

Mother: We just moved here. Our old library was always open when we needed it—even Sundays. This is such a beautiful library—it never occurred to me the library might not be open.

LSS: I know. We hear that a lot. But it's not the library's fault. The voters approved a new building, but they voted against more funds to keep it open! Of course, there wouldn't be a problem if it weren't for that stupid tax cap.

Mother *(annoyed):* What's that?

LSS: Well, it means that even though we've got all these new people moving in, building big new houses, we can't collect more tax revenues—at least not as much as we need to stay open.

Mother: Well, as far as I'm concerned, the tax cap is a good thing. Everybody always wants more money. Property owners can't afford to keep paying more and more.

LSS: That seems to be what everyone thinks. That's why the library's not open.

Mother: Well, I think you need to learn to manage your money better! You shouldn't be building expensive new buildings and then have them closed half the time.

LSS *(resigned tone):* I'm sorry you're upset, but there's not a lot I can do. I just put the books on the shelves.

Mother *(frustrated):* Well, you all need to get your act together and do something!

Scenario V: Unhappy Mom—Right Way

In this script, the mother is still upset, but the Library Super Salesperson is obviously better prepared and takes a different tack. The mother arrives agitated, but leaves in better spirits.

Mother *(angry tone):* I just have to tell someone. I am *so* upset!!! My son had a paper due today, but when we came to the library yesterday, it was closed. I couldn't believe it. How could the library not be open on Sunday????

LSS *(rises to speak. Open face and body, concerned tone):* I'm sorry. We'd like to be open more hours, but the money just isn't there. Do you know about our website? It's got some great resources for homework.

Mother: Actually, we just moved here. Our old library was always open when we needed it—even Sundays. This is such a beautiful library—it never occurred to me the library might not be open!

LSS *(stays open, positive):* It is too bad. We'd love to be open but we just don't have the money.

Mother *(annoyed):* Well, why not? You had money to build a new library.

LSS: Well, the voters realized our community needed a new library and approved a construction bond. But they didn't approve more operating funds to run a bigger library. Our community keeps growing, and we have a lot more people to serve, but our funding hasn't kept up. We'd like to be open Sundays—Fridays, too.

Mother: Well, I think you need to learn to manage your money better! You shouldn't be building expensive new buildings and then have them closed half the time.

LSS: I understand your concern. Actually, we got a really good deal on the building. And believe me, we're stretching every dollar. But with a little more money, we could offer a lot more service. We're hoping that when the new shopping mall is built, we might get some of those tax dollars. You might want to let your council representative know if you think this is a good idea.

Mother: Well, I do hope you do get some more money . . .

LSS: Do you know about our Friends of the Library? They're people like you who care about the library. Let me give you this brochure. Also, here's a bookmark with our hours and the URL. See you soon!

Buzz Grant Project Background

Why do libraries need word-of-mouth marketing (WOMM)?

A 2005 survey conducted by the Illinois Library System Director's Organization (ILSDO) asked librarians to identify the trend that kept them up at night. The majority of respondents wanted help in demonstrating their value to the general public. The 2005 OCLC study "Perceptions of Libraries and Information Resources" complemented the findings of the ILSDO survey. The study revealed that the majority of the general public do not know about all the resources libraries offer. A startling conclusion states, "Overall, not knowing the [library] website exists is the main reason respondents do not use the library website."

This information, as well as the personal experiences of library staff, reinforces the fact that libraries are not creating enough meaningful buzz about their programs and services. The corporate world is full of success stories attributed to word-of-mouth marketing. Research has shown that, first and foremost, people are influenced by information from known or trusted individuals over other types of traditional advertising.

This LSTA grant was created with the following anticipated outcomes:

- Library staff will be more familiar with buzz marketing techniques.
- Library staff will generate ideas for using these techniques with the general public.
- Library staff will plan and implement a specific buzz marketing activity.
- Library customers will have a greater realization of library services and resources.

Funding for this grant was provided by the Illinois State Library, a Division of the Office of the Secretary of State, using federal LSTA funding.

GRANT ACTIVITIES AND METHODS

The grant, which was conducted as a partnership of the DuPage Library System (DLS) and the North Suburban Library System (NSLS), provided training, planning support, and informational resources for libraries of all types. Full grant participation included thirty-five libraries (thirteen from DLS; twenty-two from NSLS). The breakout by library type: three academic, twenty-nine public, two school, and one special.

Peggy Barber and Linda Wallace, of Library Communication Strategies (LCS), were hired as consultants to lead the training sessions and provide individualized guidance for libraries for project development.

Two library programs were presented in January 2007. The first was a basic training session led by LCS. It was open to all libraries regardless of further participation in the grant.

January–March

Each participating library developed a WOMM project plan. LCS reviewed all plans and worked with libraries via e-mail, phone, and in-person visits on development of their projects. Grant participants, systems staff, and LCS began to share information on the Buzz Grant Community of Practice (an online forum). Each library and system received one copy of three marketing books purchased for the grant.

April–June

Each library implemented its project and completed consultation sessions with LCS. A number of libraries had LCS present special programs on WOMM to staff and boards to help them understand the concept and enhance their skills.

June

Two wrap-up sessions were held for participating libraries to share details of their projects.

August

Participating libraries submitted a written summary of their project based on a template provided by the two regional systems. These were submitted electronically, and many included electronic files of marketing materials created to support the library project. Reports and marketing samples are posted on the grant website, at www.nsls.info/buzzmarketing/.

September

A Buzz Expo, consisting of presentations and exhibits from a number of participating libraries, was presented on September 7, 2007.

PROJECT OUTCOMES

Over and over, libraries commented that staff education turned out to be the key component in producing a successful project, and in a number of cases, this was the project. Most of the libraries focused on staff training that involved both a greater understanding of the need for marketing and education on library services. Libraries learned the power of inclusion. When supplied with technical training, talking points, and a greater understanding of the impact of positive human interaction to the "bottom line," staff had surprising success with WOMM.

Libraries became educated on the need for all staff to be part of the marketing effort, and they really began to embrace it. One library told how their most introverted staff member surprisingly turned out to be a super library salesperson. This person was able to do so with good training and a thorough understanding of the WOMM plan prepared by the library. Libraries also became aware and accepting of the lesson that success will come only if they start with a good plan, and then follow it.

Spurred on by their success, many libraries have commented that they will use WOMM for new efforts or to continue ones started with the grant. Many found success that had long eluded them, and they exhibited great relief and enthusiasm for finally "cracking that nut."

For more information, contact the project coordinators:

Judy Hoffman (jhoffman@nsls.info)
Renee Anderson (randers@dupagels.lib.il.us)
Denise Zielinski (dzielins@dupagels.lib.il.us)

Index

Note: Page numbers followed by *f* indicate figures.